THOMAS
MORE

THOMAS MORE

A very brief history

JOHN GUY

First published in Great Britain in 2017

Society for Promoting Christian Knowledge
36 Causton Street
London SW1P 4ST
www.spck.org.uk

Paperback edition published 2019

British Library Cataloguing-in-Publication Data
A catalogue record for this book is available from the British Library

ISBN 978–0–281–07738–0 (hardback)
ISBN 978–0–281–07617–8 (paperback)
eBook ISBN 978–0–281–07618–5

Typeset by Graphicraft Limited, Hong Kong
First printed in Great Britain by Ashford Colour Press
Subsequently digitally printed in Great Britain

eBook by Graphicraft Limited, Hong Kong

Produced on paper from sustainable forests

Contents

Acknowledgements

I gladly acknowledge the kindness of archivists and curators at the British Library, the National Archives, Cambridge University Library, the Heinz Archive and Library, the National Portrait Gallery, the Royal Collection, the Frick Collection, New York, and the superlative London Library. I'm especially grateful to Jenny Delves, archivist of the Diocesan Archives, Archdiocese of Southwark, who quickly located the boxes of documents I needed and allowed me to read them in the splendour of the archbishop's dining-room in November 2015. An early version of Chapter 6 on 'Thomas More in art' was first read as a conference paper at the University of Warwick in April 2009, and I warmly thank the organizers and those members of my audience who offered comments. I've now worked on Thomas More, on and off, since I was a student in Cambridge of Sir Geoffrey Elton: this short book will positively be my last word on the subject. I very much doubt I'd have written it had not Philip Law of SPCK Publishing approached me at exactly the right moment. The obvious appeal was the opportunities the commission gave me to reflect on the enduring significance of *Utopia* during the book's 500th anniversary year and to research, for the very first time, the remarkable circumstances of More's canonization in 1935.

I must warmly thank all those in the fields of Tudor History and Renaissance Studies with whom I've worked in Cambridge, London, Bristol, St Andrews and the USA,

Acknowledgements

both colleagues and students. As always my greatest debt is to Julia for her help and constant support. I can never adequately thank her or repay her love.

John Guy

Chronology

1478 (6 February)	Probable birth date (other possible dates, 6/7 February 1477 or 7 February 1478)
c.1490	A page in the household of Cardinal Morton
c.1492	At Oxford University
c.1494	A law student at New Inn
1496	Admitted to Lincoln's Inn
c.1501–3	Lectures to law students; lives in or about the London Charterhouse
1504 (January)	Sits in the House of Commons
c.1504 (November)	Marries Joanna (or Jane) Colt
1505–6	Erasmus stays with More at Bucklersbury
1509 (March)	Admitted to the Mercers' Company
1509 (October)	Erasmus begins *The Praise of Folly* at More's house
1510 (3 September)	appointed an undersheriff of London
1511	Joanna More dies; More marries Alice Middleton
c.1513–21	Writes the 'History of King Richard III'
1514	Lent Reader at Lincoln's Inn
1515 (May)	Sent to Bruges on the embassy which begins *Utopia*
1516 (spring)	Resumes writing *Utopia* in London
1517 (1 May)	Evil May Day

Chronology

1518 (March)	Sworn in as a king's councillor
1518 (23 July)	Resigns as undersheriff of London
c.1519	Becomes one of Henry VIII's secretaries, soon acting as principal secretary
1521 (2 May)	Appointed under-treasurer of the exchequer and knighted
1521 (spring)	Helps Henry with his *Assertio Septem Sacramentorum*
1523 (15 April)	Elected Speaker of the House of Commons
1523	Writes the *Answer to Luther*
1524	Buys estate at Chelsea
1525 (summer)	Helps Wolsey to negotiate an Anglo-French entente
1525 (29 September)	Appointed chancellor of the duchy of Lancaster
1526 (January)	Raids the German Steelyard in search of Lutheran books and Bible translations
1526 (autumn)	Holbein arrives at More's house in Chelsea
1526 (December)	Publishes *Letter in Reply to Martin Luther*, written jointly with Henry
1527 (July–September)	With Wolsey at Amiens to ratify Anglo-French peace
1527 (12–17 October)	First consulted by Henry about the divorce
1528 (7 March)	Commissioned by Tunstal to refute Lutheran and other heretical books
1529 (June)	Publishes *Dialogue Concerning Heresies*

1529 (July–August)	At Cambrai for a peace treaty between France, Spain, the Holy Roman Empire and England
1529 (17 October)	Wolsey ousted as lord chancellor
1529 (25 October)	More appointed lord chancellor
1531 (February)	Henry requires the Convocation of Canterbury to grant him the title of 'Supreme Head of the English Church', which is granted with the qualification 'as far as the law of Christ allows'
1532 (15 May)	Convocation agrees not to convene or legislate without Henry's prior consent
1532 (16 May)	Resigns as lord chancellor
1532 (December)	Anne Boleyn is pregnant
1533 (January)	Henry marries Anne Boleyn
1533 (April)	*Apology* published. Act in Restraint of Appeals passed by Parliament
1533 (May)	Cranmer annuls Katherine of Aragon's marriage
1533 (1 June)	More refuses to attend Anne Boleyn's coronation
1533 (November)	*Debellation of Salem and Bizance* published
1534 (13 April)	Refuses the oath of succession before royal commissioners at Lambeth
1534 (17 April)	Sent to the Tower, where he begins writing *A Dialogue of Comfort against Tribulation* and other devotional works

Chronology

1534 (November)	Parliament approves Acts of Supremacy and Treason
1535 (12 June)	Richard Rich and More discuss the power of popes and Parliaments in the Tower
1535 (17 June)	Trial of Fisher
1535 (22 June)	Execution of Fisher
1535 (26 June)	Special commissioners appointed to try More
1535 (1 July)	Trial at Westminster Hall
1535 (6 July)	Executed on Tower Hill
1551	Ralph Robinson's translation of *Utopia* published
1557 (April)	William Rastell publishes the great folio edition of More's *English Works*
*c.*1556	Nicholas Harpsfield is commissioned to write More's official biography
*c.*1556	William Roper writes his biography of More
1582–3	Cults of Fisher and More as martyrs implicitly approved by Pope Gregory XIII
1584	Engraving of a fresco depicting the martyrdoms of Fisher and More published at Rome
1588	Stapleton's *Tres Thomae* published at Douai
1626	Roper's *Life, Arraignment and Death of that Mirror of All True Honour and Virtue, Sir Thomas More* published at St Omer

1684	Burnet's *Utopia Translated into English* published
1886 (29 December)	Pope Leo XIII beatifies Fisher and More
1918	Obelisk including More's name is sculptured on Lenin's orders and unveiled in Moscow's Alexandrovsky Gardens
1935 (19 May)	Pope Pius XI canonizes Fisher and More
1977/1978	500th anniversary of More's birth is celebrated by exhibitions and conferences in London, Dublin, Angers, New York and Washington DC
1999 (14 January)	Congressman Henry Hyde cites More at the opening of President Clinton's impeachment trial
2000 (31 October)	Pope John Paul II proclaims More the patron saint of politicians and people in public life
2016 (*c.*15 December)	500th anniversary of the publication of *Utopia*

Part 1

THE HISTORY

1

Shaping a mind

The boy who would grow up to write *Utopia* and afterwards defy Henry VIII over his break with the papacy was born in Milk Street, off Cheapside near St Paul's in London, probably on Friday, 6 February 1478. Named Thomas after Thomas Becket, the twelfth-century archbishop of Canterbury who had been bludgeoned to death in his cathedral by armed knights during vespers for opposing King Henry II, he was the second child and eldest son of John More, then a barrister, later a judge. His mother was Agnes Graunger, a London merchant's daughter.

John More yearned for his son to be a lawyer like himself. He sent Thomas to learn the rudiments of English and Latin grammar at St Anthony's School in Threadneedle Street, a short distance from Cheapside, and then found him a place at Lambeth Palace on the opposite bank of the Thames as a page in the household of Cardinal Morton, King Henry VII's trusted councillor, archbishop of Canterbury and lord chancellor. One of the age's most influential movers and shakers, Morton also held the post of chancellor of Oxford University, where Thomas More went to study when just 14 or 15. John More agreed to this, but insisted that his son should not stay for longer than a couple of years.

For all his bonhomie and love of practical jokes, the elder More was a man of steel. Around 1494 when his son was 16, he ordered him back to London. After two years studying at New Inn off the Strand, Thomas was admitted to Lincoln's Inn in Holborn, where he embarked on the rigorous course of readings, lectures and moots that would prepare him for his legal career.

In Oxford, however, Thomas had encountered William Grocyn, an inspirational teacher with a passion for the new ancient Greek learning that had reached England from northern Italy. Under Morton's guidance, Oxford was becoming a centre for the Renaissance-inspired curriculum known as the liberal arts. Thomas seems to have attended Grocyn's divinity lectures, famous for using the earliest, most authentic Greek sources to rewrite the early history of Christianity and expose the errors in the Latin versions of several key texts. To prepare himself, Grocyn spent three years mastering ancient Greek, chiefly in Florence, where he took under his wing a younger Oxford man, Thomas Linacre, a physician studying mainly in Padua and Venice and needing Greek for his research into Galen's writings.[1]

After leaving Oxford, Thomas More obediently threw himself into his legal training – until, first, Grocyn was appointed vicar of the parish church of St Lawrence Jewry beside Guildhall in London where the More family worshipped, and then Linacre took a house close by, some 50 yards from St Paul's. Within a few months, Thomas More had fallen under their spell and was embarking eagerly on a study of Greek poetry before switching to history and moral philosophy.

Joining them was John Colet, son of a wealthy mercer twice lord mayor of London. He had lived for a while in Rome and Florence and was lecturing in Oxford and London on the epistles of St Paul. Always better equipped as a philosopher than a linguist, Colet brought a fresh pair of eyes to the 'Greek project' on which his friends had embarked. Soon they imagined themselves to be explorers on a voyage of discovery equal to anything achieved by Christopher Columbus or Amerigo Vespucci in the New World. Their notion of progress depended on rediscovering the best ideas of the ancient Greek world and then improving their own society by applying those values to their own times.

A purely chance encounter, one that changed Thomas More for ever, took place in the summer of 1499. William Blount, Lord Mountjoy, the son-in-law of a neighbour of the More family at Gobions, their country estate near North Mimms in Hertfordshire, introduced Thomas and his friends to his tutor at the University of Paris, the maverick genius Erasmus of Rotterdam, who was visiting London. The most illustrious champion of the liberal arts north of the Alps, Erasmus saw that Grocyn's methods could be applied not merely to church history, but to transforming the text of the New Testament. Soon Erasmus would be carefully deciphering, collating and editing as many of the Greek manuscripts of the Gospels as he could find, before translating them into fluent, colloquial, accurate Latin. He intended to publish the Greek text and his translation on facing pages so that anyone could easily compare them and draw their own conclusions.

In 1501, Thomas qualified as a barrister, after which he earned a living by lecturing to first-year students preparing for admission to the inns of court. His ambition for a conventional lawyer's career had flagged, much to the irritation of John More, who resented what he always regarded as the malign influence of Erasmus, someone he judged to be a dangerously overeducated scrounger. Later, Erasmus reflected that Thomas as a younger man:

devoted himself to the study of Greek literature and philosophy, with so little support from his father ... that his
efforts were deprived of all outside help and he was treated
almost as if disinherited because he was thought to be
deserting his father's profession.[2]

The result was a family quarrel. Thomas More left his father's
house, moving to West Smithfield to live among the
Carthusian monks, in or about the grounds of the Charterhouse on a site surrounded by gardens, fields and burial
pits about 20 minutes' walk from Lincoln's Inn. There
he tested his vocation for the priesthood – not that he
withdrew completely from the world, for he continued to
teach his students, and he returned to Grocyn's church to
deliver a series of well-attended lectures on St Augustine's
City of God. The legend is that he wanted to be a priest or
monk, but sex got in the way.

Thomas certainly enjoyed the company of women: one
of his Latin poems, written when he was 41, expressed his
delight at fleetingly seeing again a woman with whom
he had fallen madly in love when he was 16.[3] That said, the
idea that he was a 'failed monk' who spent the rest of
his life attempting to atone for his moral weakness is ill
conceived.[4] His departure from the Charterhouse, rather,
reflected his intention to seek political engagement in the
world: we should imagine him as a lawyer who loved justice
more than he liked lawyers, living at a time of rapid social
and economic change. Most lawyers took the view that
English law, based as it was on customs and principles
dating back to Magna Carta, already served the common
welfare and should not be changed. Thomas profoundly
disagreed. He had come to think that the best way to
improve society was not to retreat to a life of prayer and

contemplation in the cloister, but to confront life's chal-
lenges as an active citizen of a Christian commonwealth.
In reaching this conclusion, the biggest challenge he faced
was himself. Always able to see both sides of the question,
his Charterhouse years were when he realized that, at heart,
he might always be something of a divided consciousness.

Thomas must have left the Charterhouse by January 1504,
because he took his seat as a member of the House of Commons then. It all went horribly wrong: he came to Henry
VII's attention in the worst possible way by speaking out
against royal taxation. After that frightening brush with
power, he kept his head down and, to his father's delight,
concentrated on his legal practice. According to Erasmus,
'there was no one whose advice was more freely sought by
litigants', and Thomas found himself able to command substantial fees.[5] He quickly married, choosing Joanna (or Jane)
Colt, the eldest daughter of Sir John Colt of Netherhall,
near Roydon in Essex. The families were already acquainted,
and Roydon was within easy riding distance of Gobions.

After the wedding, in or around November 1504, Thomas
leased The Barge at Bucklersbury, a large, rambling stone
and timber dwelling with an enormous garden in the parish
of St Stephen Walbrook, off the east end of Cheapside, close
to the Stocks Market where meat, poultry and fish were
sold. When the newlyweds first moved in, they had a lease
for only a part of the property: it took Thomas eight years
before he could afford a 40-year lease of the whole site.
His four children, three girls and a boy, were born there,
and a foster-sister was adopted as a playmate for his eldest
daughter, Margaret.

In 1505–6, when Erasmus came to stay, he and Thomas
amused one another by translating the dialogues and

declamations of Lucian of Samosata, a second-century Greek writer whose sharp wit and cutting satire were the closest thing the two friends could find to their own ideal of humour. Trenchant, pithy, caustic, the master of derision, Lucian punctured pride and pretension by showing that the worst of the pretenders were priests and politicians. Always something of a jester with a love of 'merry tales', Thomas would later in life describe himself 'of nature even half a giglet and more. I would I could as easily mend my fault as I well know it.'[6] (A 'giglet' is someone excessively prone to jesting and merriment.)

In these months, Thomas drafted a particularly fine speech in reply to Lucian's *The Tyrannicide* in which a citizen claims to deserve the city's reward for killing a tyrant. More's reply, addressed to the same fictional jurymen, reveals his loathing of tyranny, which he sees as inexorably rooted in human nature, but also his obedience to law and legitimate authority. His main conclusion is that a wise politician must have an accurate knowledge of the true roots of political disease before he can hope to cure it. Assassination is never likely to be the solution to tyranny.

Two months after More's thirty-first birthday in 1509, the teenage Henry VIII succeeded as king. By way of homage, Thomas presented him with a handsomely illustrated set of verses celebrating his coronation and marriage to Katherine of Aragon. The verses ended with a eulogy of Katherine, whom Thomas had admiringly watched riding in procession after her first arrival in London to marry Henry's elder brother, Arthur, who had died in 1502. More, who, in the company of Erasmus and a fellow law student, had first been introduced to Henry in 1499 when they paid a visit to the royal schoolroom at Eltham Palace, regarded his accession as a joyous turning-point. Thomas in his verses praised his new sovereign's looks, intellect, physical prowess and respect for justice and the rule of law. In a calculated risk, he said the young king had banished fear and oppression ('Only ex-informers fear informers now') – tantamount to an open rebuke of Henry VII's methods, but exactly what his son wanted to hear.[7]

Was Thomas already looking to Henry as a possible future employer and to himself as a royal councillor? Was this the way he believed he might put into practice the more abstract ideas he had spent so long discussing with Grocyn, Linacre and Colet? Outwardly, he denied the charge. Already, though, he was serving as a legal adviser or arbitrator in high-profile disputes between Londoners and wealthy foreign merchants. In recognition, the Mercers' Company had recruited him as one of their honorary members. When in September 1509 the 'pensionary' or chief city clerk of Antwerp visited London to settle some commercial disputes, he made his first grand entrance into Mercers' Hall to find Thomas waiting to greet him in elegant, fluent Latin, ready to open negotiations on behalf of the English merchant adventurers.

More's career took another leap forward a year later, when he was appointed an undersheriff of London, a permanent official who advised the sheriffs and sat as judge in the sheriff's court. The undersheriffs received a generous stipend, but they also had a lucrative right to represent the City in the royal courts at Westminster. Meanwhile, Thomas found himself drawn into a variety of other special tasks. He assisted the staff of the court of chancery as a part-time examiner and arbitrator. He became the link man between the City and the royal Court after Henry declared war on France in 1512. One of his earliest responsibilities was to oversee the provision by the London bakers of the huge quantities of dry biscuit needed for Henry's navy. Soon he would be meeting royal councillors regularly 'for divers causes' on the City's behalf.

In the summer of 1511, More's wife Joanna died at the age of 23, most likely in childbirth. Within a month he had married a wealthy widow seven years older than himself. His new wife was Alice, widow of John Middleton, a wool exporter and mercer based in Fenchurch Street, whom he had known for almost 20 years. The speed of his remarriage made Thomas the subject of gossip, but the evidence is undisputed. John Bouge, More's confessor, later a Carthusian monk, wrote:

> [Thomas] was my parishioner at London. I christened him two goodly children. I buried his first wife. And within a month after, he came to me on a Sunday, at night late, and there he brought me a dispensation to be married the next Monday, without any banns asking.[8]

The fact is that Alice was sassy and redoubtable, a woman already past the age of childbearing who loved to joke and banter with Thomas, and he with her. Erasmus, who stayed at Bucklersbury for a second time in 1509–10 (it was then that he wrote and dedicated to More his coruscating critique of all that was wrong in the Church and the monasteries, *The Praise of Folly**), kept away once Alice was in charge. In letters to his friends, Erasmus depicted her as loud, bossy and ignorant, more fishwife than lawyer's wife. For all that, she was at ease with herself and the world, taking charge of Thomas's household and his children from the moment

---

* In Latin *Moriae encomium*, a pun on Thomas's name.

she arrived, an arrangement that clearly suited them both
well.

It was a highly sensitive star chamber case, begun in the
spring of 1514, concerning an impounded cargo of alum
belonging to Pope Leo X that propelled Thomas most conspicuously into the limelight in these years and encouraged
the great Cardinal Wolsey, Henry's first chief minister, to
single him out as a high flyer. The case arose after the Duke
of Suffolk, Henry's favourite jousting partner, seized 4,000
barrels of alum valued at 12,000 ducats at Southampton.
An essential fixer of dyes for wool, silk and linen fabrics,
alum came from the papal mines at Tolfa, near Rome. Leo
wanted to recover and sell it, and the mayor and aldermen
of London became parties to the litigation as a result of a
long-running dispute with the pope's factor. Called upon
to act as a translator and adviser to the pope's accredited
nuncio, More found himself walking on eggshells. After
deadlock lasting almost a year, he finally proposed an out-
of-court settlement, one so fair and rational that everyone
accepted it on the spot. Leo was delighted, and so were
Henry and Wolsey.

So it was hardly surprising that in May 1515 Thomas
was selected to join an embassy that Henry and Wolsey
were sending to Bruges to treat with the advisers of Charles
of Castile, Duke of Burgundy. Led by Cuthbert Tunstal,
another of Grocyn's protégés who was already working
for Wolsey, the delegation was charged with renewing the
Anglo-Burgundian amity and confirming the treaties that
protected the Anglo-Flemish wool and cloth trades. But the
career-diplomats needed the help of commercial specialists,
and More was chosen along with John Clifford, the governor of the merchant adventurers. When in July, however,

the diplomats were summoned separately to Brussels, More was left kicking his heels for the rest of the summer, free to amuse himself as he chose. And with time on his hands, he decided to turn his mind to something different.

Thomas first met up with Erasmus, then in Flanders on his way from London to Basel in Switzerland, who recommended that he visit Antwerp and seek out Peter Gillis, a civic official who performed duties similar to More's as undersheriff. Just eight years younger than Thomas, Gillis was another fluent linguist with a passion for Greek literature. Deciding to make the trip, More was invigorated by his encounters with Gillis and by the sights and bookshops of Antwerp, a hub of world trade and finance, and the gateway to the Portuguese and Spanish territories in the East Indies and the New World. A vibrant, racially diverse metropolis with a large foreign merchant population, the city thrived on rumours and travellers' tales about ships and storms and fortunes to be made in strange lands, whether true or fictional.

It was in this setting that *Utopia* would find its beginnings. The book started life, said its author, as a series of conversations with Peter Gillis in a grassy arbour at his lodgings in Antwerp just like the one Thomas had constructed for his own family in his garden at Bucklersbury. The result would be a work of disruptive energy and singular imagination, a literary masterpiece.

2

Utopia

Inspired by his conversations with Peter Gillis, Thomas More produced the little book he called *On the Best State of a Commonwealth and on the New Island of Utopia*, soon to be known by the short title of *Utopia*, in two stages.[1] Writing in Latin, then still a living language, he began over the summer months of 1515 while in Flanders with what is now the opening of Part I and almost all of Part II. The rest was fitted into spare moments during the spring and summer of 1516, after he had returned to London. The work opens in a factual vein with a brief account by More of his mission to Bruges and excursion to meet Peter Gillis. He then goes on to say that, after mass one day at the cathedral of Notre Dame in Antwerp, he met Gillis in the company of a Portuguese traveller, Raphael Hythloday, a heavily bearded, sunburned man with a long cloak hanging loosely from his shoulders. With Hythloday's entry into the conversation, More slips seamlessly from fact into fiction.

He identifies Hythloday (whose name in Greek means 'purveyor of nonsense') as a ship's captain who had travelled with Amerigo Vespucci on three of his voyages to the New World, and who had gained Vespucci's permission to be one of 24 men who stayed behind at the farthest point of the last voyage, afterwards travelling with five companions through many countries until he reached the west coast of India. Hythloday, though, is no ordinary sailor. As Gillis points out, his sailing has been more like that of Plato. Hythloday, it appears, intends to take us on a voyage of discovery into the conceptual world of moral philosophy. As the author of the *Republic* or a description of an ideal commonwealth, Plato, like Thomas More, was on a quest for the perfect society. In Plato's ancient Greek scheme of values, however, the supreme social ideals of 'justice' and 'equality' were made possible only by the strict regulation of wealth. The contrast with More's own society, traditionally motivated more by Roman-inspired values of glory, honour, ambition and private property, could not have been greater.

To hold our attention, Thomas gives his readers more than a playful hint that ingenious 'nonsense' will be part of the fun. Almost everything Hythloday is about to describe turns out to be coined from Greek words implying nonsense or non-existence.[2] More invents the name of the 'new island' of Utopia where people live in an idyllic state of nature by fusing the Greek *ού* meaning 'not' or 'in no manner' with *topos* or 'place'. Utopia is 'no place', but also a pun on another Greek compound (*εύ-topia*) meaning 'fair', 'fortunate' or 'good place'. The title of its governor is Ademus, an official 'without people'. The river Anyder is 'waterless' and it flows through the capital Amaurot, the 'dark' or 'unknown city'. The people known as the Polylerites whom Hythloday had encountered in his travels are 'the people of much nonsense'. Writing to Erasmus in September 1516 enclosing the manuscript of *Utopia*, knowing that his friend could be relied on to arrange for its publication, More explained gleefully, 'I am sending you my *Nusquam* ("Nowhere"), which is nowhere well written.'[3] His use of the Latin word *nusquam*, not *Utopia*, as we might have expected, makes explicit what anyone with a rudimentary knowledge of Greek would have grasped: the island of Utopia exists only in the imagination, and the story, while presented as fact, is actually fiction.

And yet Hythloday is also deadly serious. For the remainder of *Utopia*, he engages in conversation an interlocutor known as 'Thomas More', a character who most likely represents one side of Thomas More's divided consciousness, the side that sought political engagement, while Hythloday represents the side that favoured study and contemplation set apart from the bustle of the world. It follows that what Hythloday recounts may turn out to be nonsense only from a particular point of view – that of 'Thomas More'. Very likely, More is enjoying a joke at his own expense. For the name 'More' is itself a significant pun. *Utopia*'s readers could hardly forget Erasmus's *Praise of Folly* with its dedication to More, a book in which lacerating wisdom is spoken from the mouth of a character called 'Moria' or 'Folly'. Already, therefore, the structure of *Utopia* suggests that Hythloday's advice, when looked at from a specific viewpoint (that of 'Thomas More'), can look like 'nonsense', but if it can be considered on its merits may still yield 'the best state of a commonwealth'.[4]

In More's first draft of the book, Hythloday began his account of Utopian society without further preliminaries. Their island, he says, is made up of 54 cities, identical in language, institutions and laws. Ruled on republican principles, the Utopians have abolished professional lawyers and private property, considering this to be the best way to uproot pride and greed. Each city contains around 6,000 households, each with no fewer than 10 and no more than 16 adults. Everything is held in common. Money is needed for trade with foreign cities, but in practice such transactions are handled on the basis of promissory notes. The Utopians need gold reserves only to lend to other nations or in time of war. With a Lucianic twist that had Erasmus splitting his sides with laughter when he read it, Hythloday goes on to report that they consider gold and silver to be inferior to iron. So little do they value gold, they use it to manufacture urinals and the chains and shackles of slaves. Notorious criminals are forced to wear gold rings in their ears and on their fingers, and even golden headbands. Rather than flaunt their prosperity as most wealthy Europeans do, the Utopians eat from earthenware dishes and drink from glass beakers.

Everyone has to work in Utopia. Farms operate on a collective basis, directing labour and resources to where they are most needed, especially at harvest time. Farming provides a job for everyone, men and women alike, but since no one lives by bread alone, everyone also learns a trade or handicraft. The working day is fixed at six hours to leave sufficient time for leisure. Some magistrates are exempt from manual labour, but rarely avail themselves of the privilege. Intellectuals are generally excused so that they may devote all of their working hours to study, but those failing to achieve their potential are reassigned to normal duties.

The Utopians dress simply and without ostentation: their clothes are made of undyed wool like the habits of Carthusian monks. And their society is unashamedly patriarchal. Wives act as servants to their husbands, children to their parents, and the young to their elders. Women are treated 'equally', but in reality are governed by their husbands. They also work harder – More seems oblivious to this point – since their duties include cooking and childcare as well as manual labour. Even in Utopia, it seems, working women have two jobs.

Health and educational provisions, though, are well ahead of their time. Every city has four hospitals and as many physicians and nurses as are needed, all working shifts to ensure fully qualified staff are on call day and night. The Utopians care lovingly for the sick and spare nothing in the way of medicine or diet to restore patients to health. In a similar vein, every child receives a free education. Pupils are first taught to read and write, before progressing to more advanced subjects. For adults there are daily public lectures before dawn, compulsory for the intellectuals, optional for the rest. Hythloday is impressed that so many Utopians flock to attend.

The Utopians understand human weaknesses well enough to know that the love of money is the root of all evil. By their application of reason, they are able to discriminate between true and false values. They have no place for hollow spectacle, courtly gesture, a social hierarchy or empty titles of honour. Inherited wealth and social status are alien to them. The only status distinctions they allow arise from intellectual ability, election to public office or punishment for crime. Foolish sports like hunting or gambling are banned, as are wine bars and brothels. Secret meetings are forbidden, since no space must exist for political conspiracy. Leisure time is organized so as to cultivate the liberal arts – for relaxation, most Utopians like to read, stroll in their gardens, make music or enjoy improving board games.

The Utopians are pacifists who think war is an activity fit only for beasts. They go to war only for defensive reasons or to liberate an oppressed people from tyranny. As soon as war is declared, they infiltrate enemy territory and post placards promising large rewards to anyone who will assassinate the enemy prince. When they need to fight, they commit their own citizens sparingly and spend their gold reserves on hiring foreign mercenaries. Since they pay the highest rates, they get the best soldiers. Once a war is concluded, the costs are indemnified by the conquered people, who are forced to cede not only money, but also lands from which the Utopians and their allies may enjoy permanent revenue.

There is no official Utopian religion as their society is polytheist. Despite this, they agree on one 'supreme god' whom they call 'Mithra', to whom they attribute the creation and providential government of the world. Religious toleration was prescribed by the original founder of Utopia, King Utopus.* He laid down by law that everyone may observe the religion of his or her choice and proselytize for it, providing it is done rationally and without offending others. If persuasion fails, no one may resort to violence or abuse, and anyone who fights over religion is punished by exile or slavery.

Despite his advocacy of toleration (and arguably in contradiction of it), King Utopus required conformity to two fundamental beliefs, because they affirm the dignity of human nature. The first is the doctrine of the immortality of the soul, the second a belief that the universe is ruled by divine providence and not by 'blind chance'. Although these are religious principles, the Utopians see them as derived from natural reason. They provide a necessary sanction for morality and a life of virtue. If there is no reward

---

* Utopus functions in the book as a legendary lawgiver in the style of Solon of Athens or Lycurgus of Sparta, and then swiftly disappears.

after death for virtue on earth, 'you have no compensation for having passed your entire existence without pleasure, that is, miserably'. So important were these principles to the Utopians, any citizens who challenged or denied either of them were to be stripped of their civil rights and forbidden to discuss their opinions other than privately with priests and magistrates.

The Utopians tolerate slavery, with the qualification that their slaves are merely prisoners of war, criminals or foreigners otherwise condemned to death in their own cities. With the exception of those former Utopian citizens who have resorted to crime, slaves are so generously treated in Utopia that the labouring poor from other nations voluntarily choose slavery there, preferring it to freedom in their own countries.

In Utopia euthanasia is possible, but must be entirely voluntary and is subject to the most rigorous safeguards in order to preserve human life. Other radical social provisions are less liberal than they might seem at first. Divorce is conditional and strictly controlled, and only an innocent party is permitted to remarry. Women priests are allowed, but only a widow of advanced years is ever chosen. Premarital sex is severely punished, as is seduction and attempted seduction. Adultery is punished by the harshest form of slavery. If an innocent party chooses still to love or stay married to an unfaithful spouse, this is permitted, but he or she must share in the punishment to which the guilty party is condemned.

Just as More, still in Flanders, had almost completed this version of *Utopia*, his attention was distracted by a venomous attack on Erasmus by one Martin Dorp, a newly promoted professor of theology at Leuven. Informing him that *The*

Praise of Folly had been officially censured by the university, Dorp urged Erasmus in the most unambiguous terms to abandon work on his Greek New Testament, almost ready for publication, on the grounds that anyone who dared to challenge the accuracy of the Latin Vulgate translation of the Bible made by St Jerome in AD 383 was putting the Church in danger.

Thomas More raced to his friend's defence, rushing off an 18,000-word rebuttal of Dorp's letter in a fortnight, railing against Dorp and his colleagues.[5] As the dedicatee of *The Praise of Folly*, Thomas clearly felt vulnerable himself. So vehement is his invective, so far removed from the witty, bantering style of what he had so far written of *Utopia*, that it is hard to believe they could be by the same author. Dorp's critique made More realize that if he did not take precautions, he would be next in the firing line, especially if he went on to publish *Utopia* in its present form. For Hythloday, like 'Folly', talks 'nonsense' to shake us out of our complacency. More knew that the version of *Utopia* he had before him needed to be substantially recast. As his first draft currently stood, it looked all too much as if he was saying that the heathen Utopians were so rational and so socially advanced, they were morally superior to Christian Europeans.

To deflect the charge, after he returned to London and recovered from a serious bout of sickness, More began revising *Utopia* by making additions, and then splitting his first draft into two unequal parts.[6] Hythloday's description of the island and its people became Part II and was left largely intact – except, unless he had perhaps done so before he left Flanders, More inserted a crucial passage covering the conversion of the Utopians to Christianity. The section on Utopian religion now included several paragraphs explaining how, when Hythloday and his companions showed them the Holy Scriptures, the Utopians found Christ's example and the communal way of life of his earliest followers to be so resonant of their own social gospel, they were eager to convert. Many were baptized on the spot. They could not be confirmed or given the Eucharist as those sacraments required a bishop or a priest. But the Utopians 'understand what these [sacraments] are, and eagerly desire them'. The effect is to shift the argument in Part II from a focus on 'reason' alone to a focus on 'revelation'. To achieve the ideal society, reason must be perfected by the gospel of Christ.

Next, some 14,000 words of additional text were stitched into Part I, which was set into an entirely fresh context. In this greatly expanded version, 'Thomas More' and Hythloday debate a variety of political and social ills: princely ambition, court flattery, war, the perils of standing armies, unjust laws, poverty, enclosures, theft and homicide. And they consider a possible solution: whether Hythloday, who also turns out to be an expert in Greek philosophy, should enter a royal council to champion the necessary reforms. 'Thomas More' defends political engagement, while Hythloday plays the part of the detached spirit, the uncorrupted philosopher who knows that the service of princes can only lead an honest man to a sticky end.

To clinch his point, Hythloday recounts a fable, a purported account of his experiences many years ago as a visitor in Cardinal Morton's household. At a dinner at Lambeth Palace where More had been a page, his fellow-guests, a lawyer, a flunkey and a friar, turned out to be egregious flatterers, agreeing with anything Morton might say. Hythloday, joining in their conversation, tries to show how the evils of poverty are compounded by the greed and profiteering of the rich.

The lawyer is indignant when Hythloday argues that it might be better for individuals as well as the State if petty thieves were set to work for the public good and not hanged. Hythloday advocates the merits of a system of restorative rather than retributive justice, one he says he has encountered on his many travels. His fellow-guests shake their heads – then Morton says he thinks the idea could be worth trying. It would be no riskier or more unjust, he suggests, than the retributive system. He even expands on Hythloday's suggestion: 'I think it wouldn't be a bad idea to treat vagabonds this way too, for though we've passed many laws against them, they've had no real effect as yet.'

As soon as Morton says this, the onlookers heap praise on the idea in spite of their earlier doubts. Hythloday derides them for their fawning obsequiousness, blind to the fact that Morton has given serious consideration to his proposal.

At this point 'Thomas More' seizes his opportunity. 'Your friend Plato', he tells Hythloday, 'thinks that commonwealths will be happy only when philosophers become kings or kings become philosophers. No wonder we are so far from happiness when philosophers do not condescend even to assist kings with their counsels.'

Hythloday replies that intellectuals have offered their advice through the medium of published books: the trouble is that kings always ignore them. Plato, he says, had been right to warn that kings will never be guided by wise men short of changing into philosophers themselves. Kings are inherently wilful: sleeping tyrants with no space for honest councillors.

But 'Thomas More' is ready with an answer. While conceding that 'academic philosophy' will be useless in politics, he recommends 'another philosophy more suitable for statesmen': a 'practical philosophy' that knows its place, adapts itself to the circumstances at hand, and acts its part sensitively and appropriately – like an actor playing his part on the stage, who knows when to speak his lines and when to keep silent.

Hythloday cannot agree. For an honest man to mangle the truth to make it palatable to the wicked, he contends, is insanity and the quickest way for a man to lose his head. 'At Court there is no room to dissemble or look the other way. You must openly approve the worst proposals and endorse the most vicious policies.' Anyone who seemed to give only qualified or ambivalent support to wicked counsels would be suspected as a spy, perhaps even a traitor.

At the time the real-life Thomas More wrote those words, nothing could have been troubling him more. For, on his return from Flanders, Cardinal Wolsey had conveyed to him Henry VIII's invitation to join the King's Council at a salary of £100 a year. More's career was at a crossroads. Should he accept the offer or refuse? 'Hitherto I have refused it', he reassured an anxious Erasmus,

> and it looks to me as though I should maintain my refusal. If I accepted it, I should have either to abandon my present position in London, which I prefer even to something better, or (which I should much regret) to incur some unpopularity among my fellow-citizens.[7]

All the same, the offer was alluring. He had left the Charterhouse in the belief that it was only as an active citizen in the world that he could hope to make a difference. Now he had that chance: but subsequent events would prove that he was torn in two flatly opposing directions.

3

The king's servant

Erasmus quickly arranged for More's manuscript of *Utopia* to be published at Leuven. On 15 December 1516, Thomas was impatiently awaiting his author's copies. After that, 15 whole months were to elapse before he accepted Henry VIII's offer of a place on the King's Council. In March 1518, he took his councillor's oath at Reading Abbey where the king was lodged overnight on his way to Woodstock in Oxfordshire. Henry then offered him some friendly advice, urging him to 'first look unto God and after God unto him', an interesting and perhaps unique observation, as the king is not recorded as saying this to any other newly admitted councillor. Had Wolsey already warned Henry that More had doubts about joining the murky world of politics?[1]

Thomas had won his spurs as a politician in London on May Day 1517, when over 1,000 young English-born apprentices, many unemployed, wielding axes and cudgels, looted the houses, shops and warehouses of the immigrant communities in an orgy of violence, and then released prisoners from the City's gaols. Principally, the target had been the hated money-lenders from Lombardy. Acting in his undersheriff's capacity, More had called the rioters to order. His eloquence alone, according to the chroniclers, stemmed the worst of the violence.

After law and order was speedily restored, More's value to Wolsey and Henry was self-evident. On his side, Thomas pinned his hopes for the 'best state of a commonwealth' on Wolsey, whom he judged to have the potential to become a model statesman like Cardinal Morton before him. Hythloday in *Utopia* argued that pride and greed are the chief obstacles to justice and equality. Wolsey shared many of these ideals, making 'equal' and 'impartial justice' in his courts of chancery and star chamber the mainspring of his domestic policy. Except that Wolsey's reforming forays as Henry's lord chancellor were spasmodic: short bursts of energy would be matched by lengthy periods of inertia as his attention darted elsewhere.

Quite possibly Thomas chose March 1518 as the moment to accept the call to royal service because Pope Leo X had just issued a decree for a truce among European powers that Wolsey planned to turn into a platform for a Treaty of Universal Peace. Besides giving a speech on the arrival in London of the papal nuncio sent to help negotiate the peace, More was one of the treaty's signatories.

A year or so later, Wolsey promoted Thomas to be one of Henry's secretaries. The chief minister had come to mistrust Richard Pace, the principal secretary. More, Wolsey felt, would be more dependable. Soon Thomas had taken over, travelling everywhere with Henry, on call day or night, seven days a week. He came to know the king and the workings of his mind better than anyone. And, in spite of the social gulf between them, Henry treated him as a friend. That might seem uncanny given that Henry, barely in his 30s, was a sportsman, an extrovert and a hedonist bent on enjoying himself, whereas Thomas, by now in his mid-40s, was a scholar by temperament. All the same, Henry was reasonably well read and fancied himself as an intellectual. A keen amateur theologian, mathematician and musician, and a budding astronomer, he would join More in poring over the diagrams in Thomas's copy of Euclid's *Geometry* and would burst unannounced into his room in the middle of the night, dragging Thomas on to the roofs of royal palaces to gaze at the stars. Apart from Wolsey, More was the only councillor with whom the king routinely linked arms as they strolled together around gardens or long galleries. Unlike Wolsey, though, More never took the king's friendship for granted.

In May and June 1520, Thomas accompanied Henry and Wolsey to their glittering rendezvous with King Francis I of France in the so-called 'Golden Valley', halfway between the towns of Guisnes and Ardres and known as the Field of Cloth of Gold. While everyone else was feasting, dancing or jousting, Thomas was expected to slip away to discuss secret matters with Francis's secretary. He then had the delicate task of persuading the envoys of the newly elected Holy Roman Emperor, Charles V,* that Henry's approach to European diplomacy was even-handed. After that, Wolsey sent him back to Flanders to settle more commercial disputes, this time with the merchants of the German Hanseatic League.

In August 1521, Thomas accompanied Wolsey on a delicate mission to Calais and Bruges to mediate between Francis and Charles. It would prove to be a defining moment. After ostensibly courting both sides, Wolsey made a secret bargain, pledging that Henry would invade France in alliance with Charles before two years were out. In return, Charles promised to support Wolsey for election to the papacy when it next fell vacant, a promise he spectacularly failed to keep. Thomas More saw all too clearly where this was leading: blinded by pride and ambition, Wolsey was putting his own interests ahead of those of peace and the commonwealth.

---

* Formerly Charles of Castile, Duke of Burgundy.

More dropped hints of disillusionment with Henry too. In April the same year, the king had ordered the arrest of Edward Stafford, Duke of Buckingham, whom he accused of high treason. He claimed the duke was plotting to depose him, incited by the prophecies of Nicholas Hopkins, a Carthusian monk. According to these predictions, Henry 'would have no issue male of his body' and Buckingham 'should get the favour of the commons and he should have the rule of all England'. The duke also stood accused of slandering Wolsey, calling him 'the king's bawd' for arranging the lying-in of Elizabeth Blount, Henry's mistress, when she was pregnant with the king's illegitimate son Henry Fitzroy.[2]

After a rigged trial in which the king selected the judges and coached the prosecution witnesses, forcing information out of Buckingham's chaplain and so breaking the seal of the confessional, the duke was found guilty. Sentence of death was pronounced by his fellow peer, the Duke of Norfolk, who was barely able to control his tears as he delivered the verdict. Buckingham's end was brutal. He died in agony, beheaded on 17 May by a bungling executioner who took three strokes of the axe to sever his head.

To pre-empt a popular uprising, Thomas More was sent by Henry to Guildhall to stop 'the lamenting and sorrowing' of Londoners for the duke. Traitors, he was ordered to say, should not be indulged. He had to threaten the citizens, telling them that they had incurred Henry's 'great suspicion, and he will not forget'. Forced to return four days later, More had to instruct the mayor and aldermen to put the City's constables and night-watchmen on full alert, and to seize and embargo all armour and weapons stored either at Guildhall or in people's homes until the king decided otherwise.[3] So resonant was this of Richard III's tactics after

27

he seized the throne in 1483, More found it deeply troubling. In an unfinished manuscript of a penitential exercise on the Four Last Things – death, judgement, heaven and hell – Thomas gave a graphic, fictionalized description of a 'great Duke' secretly accused of high treason and sentenced to death against the evidence in a show trial.

At the same moment, More abandoned a gloriously vivid and dramatic 'History of King Richard III' with which he had been experimenting (in Latin and English) for several years, a manuscript which, a generation later, would form the backbone of William Shakespeare's own classic play. Thomas laid down his pen at the very point where he had just written his own version of a speech in which his hero Cardinal Morton tempts the old Duke of Buckingham, Edward Stafford's father, to revolt by telling him one of Aesop's fables in which a Lion King, whose word is law, subverts and alters the law to suit himself so that he may deceive and devour the other beasts at his pleasure.[4] That Morton should have incited a revolt against the tyrant Richard, More believed, was morally justifiable, because Richard's methods were literally diabolical and by acting as he did, Morton was attempting to outwit the devil at his own game. Already, it seems, Thomas was finding himself having to recast in his head those sections of Part I of *Utopia* in which 'Thomas More' and Hythloday debate whether an honest man could enter a king's service and offer good advice, while keeping his head on his shoulders. Sometimes, dissimulation and deceit in a worthy cause might have to be part of the package.

And yet for the next six or seven years, Thomas continued to serve Henry VIII as if nothing untoward had happened. He had entered royal service, and from it there was no easy escape. In quick succession, he was given the lucrative post of under-treasurer of the exchequer and elected Speaker of the House of Commons, both held in conjunction with the principal secretaryship. His career was on a roll, enabling him to move himself and his family from their rambling old house at Bucklersbury to a fine new estate at Chelsea. By the time renovation and landscaping works were finished, the family ended up with a comfortable riverside home surrounded by gardens and orchards, along with some 80 acres of arable land and a dozen other lesser fields and farm buildings. Perhaps a third of a mile in depth and 300 to 400 yards in width, the magnificent gardens came complete with a viewing platform, set on rising ground, enjoying a breathtaking vista of the London skyline to the north-east and of the rolling Thames to the south-west.

Then Thomas's career wobbled for a while. In September 1525, he was unexpectedly demoted from his post at the exchequer and made chancellor of the duchy of Lancaster. The reasons were political. Wolsey had come under fire from his opponents in Henry's privy chamber, men like Sir William Compton, the groom of the stool, and he sought to safeguard himself by reshuffling offices and patronage. To prise Compton away from Henry, he was given More's job at the exchequer: Thomas's salary consequently dropped by more than £100 a year, or by roughly a quarter.

Shortly afterwards, Thomas was sucked ever deeper into Henry's continuing campaign against Martin Luther, the rebel German friar and university professor who in 1517 had posted his 95 theses on a church door at Wittenberg and challenged papal authority. Henry's onslaught had first visibly taken shape in a ceremony at St Paul's in May 1521, when Pope Leo X's decree excommunicating Luther was proclaimed to the sound of trumpets, a ceremony over which Wolsey presided and which culminated in a bonfire of heretical books. Bishop John Fisher had preached a sermon, censuring Luther. Anyone tempted to slumber would, however, have been aroused when Fisher gave the startling news that Henry would himself publish a book denouncing Luther.

Sitting on the platform as the bonfire was lit, More was already one of a small team of editors and ghost-writers assisting Henry with this book, entitled *Assertio Septem Sacramentorum* ('A Defence of the Seven Sacraments'). Partly encouraged by passages in Erasmus's edition of the Greek New Testament, partly by his anger at the sale of indulgences and other church abuses, Luther denied that the pope was part of the biblical Church. He claimed that salvation is a gift of God's grace through faith in Christ alone, and he went on to claim that only three of the seven Catholic sacraments had been instituted by Christ – all opinions Henry considered to be scandalously heretical. When the king insisted on defending the papal plenitude of power in his book, More quietly took him aside and asked him if this was wise. Maybe he would quarrel with the pope himself some day? But Henry was deaf to the warning, sending off a presentation copy of his book to the Vatican with a signed frontispiece depicting himself kneeling before the pope for a blessing, for which he received in return the much coveted title of 'Defender of the Faith'.

When, in 1522, Luther answered the king's *Assertio* in a vituperative tirade, Henry conscripted More and Fisher each to write a rebuttal. Fisher's *Refutation of Martin Luther* (1523) was a theological blockbuster, running to 200,000 words. More's *Answer to Luther* appeared in two separate editions and concentrated on the issue of authority in the Church. The *Answer to Luther* evolved intellectually from

More's work on the *Assertio* and logically from his duties as principal secretary, since the secretary doubled as the king's public orator and official mouthpiece as well as his amanuensis. More argued that the 'common faith of Christendom' (as he put it) transcended the opinions of individuals or national states, that 'conscience' could not be informed simply by reading Scripture alone as Luther believed: it had to fall into line with Catholic beliefs and tradition.

Thomas next helped Henry to write his *Letter in Reply to Martin Luther*, published in December 1526, a riposte to an open letter Luther had addressed directly to the king. By then, More's private reservations about Wolsey were coming more obviously to the fore. And those reservations were shared: Uberto Gambara, the papal nuncio in England, would soon be advising Pope Clement VII to strip Wolsey of all his powers, even those granted to him for life, for systematically eroding the authority of the archbishop of Canterbury, exploiting the Church's wealth for his personal benefit and rigging English diplomacy against the pope's interest, most recently by advising Henry to exclude England from an important European alliance despite massive inducements to join.[5]

But if More shared Gambara's concerns about Wolsey, he kept them to himself. In July 1527, when Thomas set out with Wolsey for Amiens in northern France on his most ambitious diplomatic mission so far, he worked strenuously to assist the chief minister in the wider cause of a pan-European peace. By then the outlook was threatening. The Ottoman Turks had captured Belgrade and marched into Hungary. At the battle of Mohács they won a famous victory and soon would be approaching the gates of Vienna. And in Italy, a maverick section of Charles V's army had mutinied and sacked Rome, murdering the citizens, raping nuns and forcing Pope Clement to flee from the Vatican through a secret tunnel to the Castel Sant'Angelo, where he signed a truce making himself Charles's prisoner.

Besides assisting Wolsey in ratifying a peace treaty with King Francis at Amiens, Thomas was also on standby at a secret rendezvous afterwards at Compiègne, where Wolsey and Francis made plans to convene a powerful group of cardinals at Avignon and take over the government of the entire Church, claiming that the pope had been incapacitated by forces beyond his control.

More's concern for the greater good of Christendom would become visibly apparent after March 1528, when Cuthbert Tunstal, now bishop of London, licensed him to read and possess illegal writings by Luther and his followers in order to refute them. Henry had stepped up his campaign against the reformers in the closing months of 1525, shortly after the first sheets of William Tyndale's translation of the New Testament came off the press at Cologne. Wolsey lit another bonfire at St Paul's in February 1526, when Robert Barnes, the most prominent English Lutheran after Tyndale, was forced to abjure and perform public penance. Also compelled to abjure were four merchants of the German Hanseatic League, importers of Luther's writings. Thomas had arrested them a few weeks before, after one of the Germans was accused of clipping English coin. Then, in May 1528, he imprisoned the prominent London draper Humphrey Monmouth, one of Tyndale's earliest patrons, after raiding his house, searching for Lutheran books but finding none.

To better focus his attention on reading and refuting the large bundle of prohibited writings that Tunstal had sent him, Thomas withdrew to Chelsea for more than a year. The result was his famous *Dialogue Concerning Heresies*, arguably his most deeply researched book. He was allowed to shut himself away at Chelsea because William Knight, a royal chaplain, had by now taken over most of the duties of Henry's principal secretary, a move that marked a significant advance on the chessboard for Wolsey's enemies.

Published in June 1529, the *Dialogue* was the first refutation of Luther and the reformers that Thomas wrote independently of Henry VIII. Rooted in purportedly real-life conversations with an interlocutor known as 'the Messenger', Thomas created a dramatic structure in which the Messenger sets forth his Lutheran beliefs, enabling More to refute them. Once again, he realized that the vital terrain was not likely to be papal authority or the sacraments, but the unity of the Church and Catholic tradition. Whereas the Messenger rejected tradition and called for the Church and the clergy to be remodelled according to the written word of the Gospels, More argued that Catholic tradition had prevailed since the time of the apostles. The Gospels may have been revealed by Christ, but Christ had not written a book. The Gospels had been preserved in the collective memory of the Church, which had collated and set forth the texts of canonical Scripture. The Church's authority was thus independent of the written word: it did not matter how many texts, apparently disproving this or that, were cited by heretics. The 'true Gospel of Christ' had been revealed to the Church before the Bible was ever compiled.

In his *Dialogue* Thomas condemned Tyndale for his inaccuracies, but expressed a fervent wish that an authorized English translation of the Bible could be made that everyone could be allowed to read. 'I would not', he protests, 'withhold the profit that one good devout unlearned layman might take by the reading [of it], not for the harm that a hundred heretics would fall in by their own wilful abusion.'[6] A true English Bible translation, he says, should be undertaken as soon as possible.

The *Dialogue* is enlivened with some of More's 'merry tales', like one about a 'whoreson' friar who as a penance asked 12 nubile young women to sleep with him, but is also littered with highly emotive passages lumping together heretics, Turks and Saracens as malignant, evil subversives, worse than pagans and pornographers. Thomas confidently defended the use of violence against the reformers: 'the burning of heretics . . . is lawful, necessary and well done'. Violence, he claims, is always necessary to restrain the 'great outrages committed against the peace and quiet of the people in sundry places of Christendom by heretics rising of a small beginning to a high and unruly multitude'. For these reasons, 'many sore punishments' had been devised for them, 'and especially by fire'.[7]

When in October 1529, however, Henry dismissed Wolsey for his lack of progress in securing the annulment of his marriage to Katherine of Aragon so that he could marry Anne Boleyn, he turned to Thomas More to be his next lord chancellor and (as the king perhaps imagined) future chief minister. It was an inspired choice and a truly catastrophic one. Although at the time of the offer, Thomas's views on Luther chimed perfectly with Henry's own, he would turn out to be the worst possible advocate for Henry's suit for a divorce. In such circumstances, would Henry prove his earlier advice to More, urging him to 'first look unto God and after God unto him', to be worthless? Was Hythloday right – that kings are indeed sleeping tyrants with no space for opinions beyond their own?

4

The dissident

Katherine of Aragon had failed to produce a living son before she entered the menopause. Henry could not believe that he himself might be at fault, and Thomas More had first discovered shortly after returning from Amiens in October 1527 that the king was in deadly earnest about divorcing her. To make things worse for Katherine, Henry had fallen head over heels in love with Anne Boleyn, who refused to sleep with him, but promised him a son if he would marry her.

Underpinning Henry's case was the prohibition on marriage to a brother's wife (Leviticus 20.21) in the Old Testament. Such unions were forbidden by this text: the penalty was the failure of lawful male heirs. Henry believed he was living in mortal sin and asked for Thomas's opinion. The king, More says, sent him to Edward Foxe, a Cambridge protégé of Anne Boleyn and her father, who was already ghost-writing the first of a series of 'books' on the divorce for Henry. Thomas read Foxe's manuscript, but was unconvinced by it. Henry then left More alone until shortly after he made him lord chancellor, when he sent for him and asked him to 'look and consider his great matter' for a second time.[1]

Henry desperately wanted the author of *Utopia* on his side: dissent irritated him and made him feel insecure. Thomas agreed to revisit the matter, and the king sent

Thomas Cranmer, the latest Boleyn recruit, to brief him. More read 'as far forth as my poor wit and learning served me', but to no avail. He returned to Henry, explaining how 'to do him service', he would 'have been more glad than of all such worldly commodities as I either then had or ever should come to', if only he could have agreed with him. And Henry, for the moment, accepted defeat, biding his time.[2]

It had chiefly been the human potential that Thomas had seen in the younger Henry that had encouraged him to enter royal service. He had stayed in post after the Duke of Buckingham's execution because, by then, he was already in too deep. After that, the spread of Lutheranism, then the divorce, swung him round: with those twin threats confronting England and Christendom, he was determined to stick in there, to try and make things better as long as he could, even if he could not make them wholly good. As he wrote to Erasmus, still living in Basel, 'the more I realize that this post involves the interests of Christendom, my dearest Erasmus, the more I hope it all turns out successfully.'[3] No longer was Thomas More a divided consciousness as he had been when writing *Utopia*, for he had come fully to endorse the views of the semi-fictional interlocutor in Part I of the book.

But More's dissent left him marginalized in the King's Council, creating space for rivals such as Foxe, Cranmer and soon Thomas Cromwell. In September 1530, Foxe and Cranmer presented Henry with a dossier showing (as they said) the 'true difference between royal and ecclesiastical power'. Its logic was simple: the pope was merely the 'bishop of Rome', whereas Henry, throughout his dominions, was rightfully 'Christ's Vicar on Earth'. George Boleyn, Anne's brother, set about finding ways to put these ideas into practice.

To this end, he joined forces with Cromwell, a self-made man who had fought in Italy as a mercenary and worked for the Frescobaldi family of merchants in Florence and London before serving Wolsey as a fixer. Cromwell believed he knew how both Parliament and Convocation (the Church's parliament) could be made to do Henry's will. And sure enough, in February 1531, George Boleyn appeared in Convocation to bludgeon the bishops into acknowledging Henry to be 'Supreme Head of the English Church' with the qualification (later to be removed) 'as far as the law of Christ allows'.

More and Fisher, for their part, battled to stem the tide. In May 1530, Thomas had successfully chivvied Henry into bringing print-censorship for the first time within the criminal jurisdiction of the court of star chamber. Over 100 titles were placed on an index of heretical books, chief among them Tyndale's translation of the New Testament. (Here More was carrying on the work he had begun in 1528 at Tunstal's behest.)

The following year, Thomas began widening the scope of his jurisdiction as lord chancellor. After he got wind that the harsh treatment of Thomas Bilney, a leading Cambridge reformer burned alive at the stake in the Lollards' Pit at Norwich, was to be brought up for debate in Parliament, he ordered a judicial review into the case. Summoning eyewitnesses and forcing them to answer his interrogatories on oath, More concluded that Bilney had been a dangerous heretic who had recanted as the fire was set.

Next, More's pursuivants captured George Constantine, an artful dodger privy to the secrets of the English Lutherans who was illegally importing Tyndale's books. Thomas put him in the stocks in his gatehouse at Chelsea. A week or two later, Constantine splintered the wooden frame and wriggled free, scaling More's garden wall and fleeing to Antwerp.

Undeterred, Thomas trapped the Lutheran lawyer James Bainham, who had been overheard calling St Thomas Becket 'a damnable traitor'. Next to be caught was Richard Bayfield, a book-dealer. Interrogated by More at Chelsea, Bayfield was handed over to the church court, which sentenced him to be burned: the fire took an abnormally long time to catch hold, and Bayfield, bound in chains, died with excruciating slowness. Another victim was John Tewkesbury, a leather-seller and Lutheran convert whom More interrogated at Chelsea. Later Thomas wrote, 'The poor wretch lieth in hell with a hot firebrand burning at his back that all the water in the world will never be able to quench.'[4]

In straining every nerve against heretics, More believed he was serving God and Henry equally. He failed to see that, at least where the king was concerned, he was standing on shifting sands. Erasmus, too, was unsympathetic. From his sanctuary in Basel, he fell into a state of denial over the reports he received of Thomas's behaviour, refusing to believe that the author of *Utopia* could have taken this turn. Twice Erasmus claimed, inaccurately, that no heretic was put to death while More was lord chancellor. Thomas later put him straight. Writing his own epitaph a year or so after his resignation as lord chancellor, he said he had been 'grievous to thieves, murderers and heretics' and wanted all his friends to know as much. 'I wrote that with deep feeling', he told Erasmus. 'I find that breed of men absolutely loathsome, so much so, that unless they regain their senses, I want to be as hateful to them as anyone can possibly be.'[5]

More resigned as lord chancellor in May 1532, a few hours after the bishops in Convocation yielded unconditionally to Henry. The chain of events precipitating the king's break with Rome began the following October with an Anglo-French summit, arranged to ratify a Treaty of Mutual Aid. Crossing to Calais with Henry, Anne Boleyn believed she had mobilized French support in Rome for the divorce after Francis danced with her during a masque. She chose this moment to sleep with Henry and quickly became pregnant. In January 1533, she and Henry were secretly (and bigamously) married. Then, in rapid succession, Cranmer was consecrated archbishop of Canterbury and Cromwell steered legislation through Parliament prohibiting all appeals to Rome.

In May, Cranmer annulled Henry's marriage to Katherine and pronounced Anne's marriage valid. Although heavily pregnant, Anne was given a magnificent coronation, the festivities lasting for five days. 'God give grace', said Thomas More anxiously when he heard that Anne was to be crowned, 'that these matters within a while be not confirmed with oaths.'[6] He saw plainly what was coming.

No longer able to influence events except by writing books, Thomas recovered much of his old composure. Now as steely as his father had been when he had ordered his son home from Oxford to begin his legal studies, he set about defending himself in print and refused a personal invitation to attend Anne's coronation. His conscience did not allow him to attend the coronation of a queen he believed to be living in adultery. He did not recognize the validity of Cranmer's annulment. He did not believe that Parliament had the power to block Katherine's appeal to Rome or to break with the pope. He continued to believe that the 'common faith of Christendom' transcended the opinions of individuals or national states, and that 'conscience' had to fall into line with Catholic beliefs and tradition. Had he not said as much in his *Answer to Luther*, written (then) at Henry's urging?

In April 1533, the same month as Parliament passed the Act in Restraint of Appeals to Rome, More published his *Apology*, swiftly followed in the autumn by the *Debellation of Salem and Bizance*. These books, superficially, were couched merely as a defence of 'the very good old and long-approved laws, both of this realm and of the whole corps of Christendom'. In reality, they were unashamedly political. For Thomas slipped in several passages subversive of Henry and his new councillors, advising 'every good Christian man and woman' to 'stand by the old, without the contrary change of any point of our old belief for anything brought up for new'. It was, he argued, their duty to 'stand to the common well-known belief of the common-known Catholic Church of all Christian people, such faith as by yourself, and your fathers, and your grandfathers, you have known to be believed'.[7]

Such an appeal to public opinion was explosive. With Anne expecting the king's male heir as she believed, Henry was more than usually jumpy. The fact that Anne's child turned out to be a girl – the future Elizabeth I – only made him more stubborn and capricious. In March 1534, he got Cromwell to push through Parliament an Act of Succession to settle the inheritance of the Crown on Anne's children with a clause requiring any subject to swear an oath affirming the 'whole effects and contents' of the Act, including a paragraph saying that Anne's marriage was legally valid. Refusal was punishable with life imprisonment and forfeiture of all property.

Summoned before royal commissioners at Lambeth on 13 April, Thomas refused to swear the oath. After carefully reading both the wording of the oath and of the Act for as long as an hour, he explained that he would willingly swear to the dynastic succession of Anne's children as that was a purely secular matter for Parliament to decide, but not to the oath as it stood.

Warned that by refusing he was opposing the 'great council of the realm' in Parliament, Thomas answered by invoking what he considered to be the higher authority of the General Council of the Church. This cut to the heart of the matter: he resolutely stuck by his opinion that the 'common faith of Christendom' transcended the opinions of individuals or national states. Arriving after dusk to reinforce the royal commissioners, Cromwell gave More a scarcely veiled threat: 'For surely', as Thomas wrote to warn his daughter Margaret, 'the king's highness would now conceive a great suspicion against me.'[8]

Twice More repeated his offer to swear to the succession alone, to no avail. He was sent to the Tower, as was Fisher, where for more than a year both were left to stew. Cromwell allowed Margaret to visit her father during the first seven months of his incarceration, hoping that she might persuade him to change his mind and take the oath in full. She found ingenious ways to send him books and paper and helped him to smuggle his writings out of the Tower. Access to paper meant that he could write letters recounting some of his experiences to family and friends, and he also worked hard on a new manuscript, *A Dialogue of Comfort against Tribulation*, which he found liberating – writing quietly in his cell perhaps reminded him of his formative years in the Charterhouse. This work could not be published until 1553, but when it was, readers would find themselves eavesdropping on adaptations of imaginary conversations as in *Utopia* or the *Dialogue Concerning Heresies*, this time set in war-ravaged Hungary during the lull between two devastating Turkish attacks.[9] Fear and death encompass everyone. A fictional Vincent ('he who overcomes') has come to visit his aged Uncle Antony on his deathbed. More plays Antony, giving advice to an audience he judged more likely to be the future victims of the 'Great Turk' Henry VIII than of the all-conquering Suleiman the Magnificent. The work is packed with 'merry tales', some an acquired taste, like one about a woman so fiendish, the devil tempts her to goad her husband into cutting off her head so that he will be hanged or another about a 'lusty lady' who vomits into her lover's face as he lies in her lap. Others are animal stories adapted from Aesop's fables.[10]

Becoming suspicious of what they might be plotting, Cromwell severely restricted Margaret's Tower visits in and after November 1534. Her father's health deteriorated rapidly as a result. Solitary confinement did not suit him: he was too gregarious for that, and began complaining of 'gravel and stone' in his kidneys and of 'cramp that grippeth me in the legs'.

Henry, meanwhile, had threatened to 'open the eyes' of those who 'are not as learned as he is, and do not know that the real power of the pope is very small'.[11] Now his impatience would be deadly. On 17 November, Parliament recognized the king as 'Supreme Head of the Church of England' without reservations or qualifications. Next, a new Treason Act made it a capital offence to threaten or defame the royal family, even by words alone, or deny Henry's title as 'Supreme Head'.

The new legislation, the most draconian of Henry's reign, was strenuously resisted: of the Treason Act, an eyewitness said there was 'never such a sticking at the passage of any act'. The Act of Supremacy was accompanied by a new oath, which More and Fisher both refused to swear. Henry sent Cromwell to persuade Thomas, whom he accused of 'obstinacy'. He commanded him on his allegiance to give a plain answer whether the Act of Supremacy was lawful or not.[12]

More refused to be drawn, adding that the Act

> is like unto a sword with two edges, for if I say that the same law were good, then it is dangerous to the soul, and if I say contrary to the said statute, then it is death to the body. Wherefore I will make thereto none other answer, because I will not be the cause of the shortening of my life.[13]

Henry decided to put the dissidents on trial for treason. Fisher, so ill and lame he could barely walk, was sentenced to death and executed in June 1535. More followed in July. On the 1st, he stood in Westminster Hall before judges hand-picked by Henry and a jury rigged by Cromwell, when he was accused of 'maliciously' depriving the king of his title of Supreme Head of the Church while debating the powers of Parliament informally with Richard Rich in the Tower.

An ambitious young barrister newly made the king's solicitor-general, Rich was a man with a query against his name. Well known to More before he had moved to Chelsea, Rich had run for civic office in London. The contest had been too close to call, until, on the eve of the vote, the king had unexpectedly intervened to pass Rich over.[14] No one knew why, but Rich believed he could guess the name of his detractor. He suspected Thomas More, then Henry's secretary.

The judges offered More a pardon if he would confess and recant, which he refused. The case against him turned on Rich's evidence. The trial records do not report the exact words Rich said in court, but it would seem likely that he committed perjury, claiming that in their conversation, More had said in so many words that Parliament could *not* make the king Supreme Head of the Church. However, a memo in Rich's own handwriting, written for Cromwell shortly after Rich had returned from the Tower, records that Thomas had stopped short of this, saying only:

> A king may be made by Parliament and a king deprived by Parliament, to which act any subject being of the Parliament may give his consent, but to the case [you have just put to me, i.e. on the Act of Supremacy] a subject cannot be bound because he cannot give his consent [in] the Parliament.

More then gave the reason: 'Although the king were accepted in England [as Supreme Head] yet most utter [foreign] parts do not affirm the same.'[15]

Thomas's remarks, admittedly, came dangerously close to crossing the line. Henry, who had come to think More's refusal to take the oath was likely to inspire others to do the same, was pressing Cromwell for a result, and the probability is that Cromwell believed what More had now said might just be enough for a conviction. In court on the day, Rich, fearing reprisals if he fluffed his lines, may well have decided to make quite sure that the jury would convict. After he gave his evidence, there was no doubt about it.

Barely had the jury returned a guilty verdict and the lord chief justice started to pass sentence, than Thomas interrupted. Invoking an obscure legal right to speak his mind at this late stage, a right he remembered from his training at Lincoln's Inn, he declared, with nothing now to lose, that his indictment, resting as it did on the authority of the Acts of Supremacy and Treason, was invalid. Speaking candidly for the very first time, he said that the Act of Supremacy was 'directly repugnant' to God's law and the beliefs of the Catholic Church. Developing his arguments in a masterly way, Thomas then gave his opinion that 'this realm, being but one member and small part of the Church' could not legislate in a manner 'disagreeable with the general law of Christ's universal Catholic Church'. A local or national law could not override the general law of Christendom in a matter of belief. The fact that there happened 'to be made in some place a law local to the contrary' made no difference. 'No more', said the former undersheriff, 'than the City of London, being but one poor member in respect of the whole realm, might make a law against an act of Parliament to bind the whole realm.'[16]

More did not shirk from attacking Henry directly, citing the king's coronation oath and suggesting that Henry had committed perjury by allowing Parliament to attack the very Church that he had sworn to defend and uphold.

After that, Thomas was a dead man. In the words of the official court transcript, he was to be dragged by horses on a hurdle to the gallows at Tyburn to be hung until almost dead, then taken down and disembowelled, his entrails burned before his eyes while he was still alive. His head was to be cut off and his body divided into four quarters, the head to be displayed on a pole wherever the king should choose.

Henry grudgingly commuted the sentence of hanging and disembowelling to one of straightforward decapitation, although More's head was still to be impaled with those of other traitors on London Bridge. Early in the morning of Tuesday, 6 July, Thomas mounted the scaffold on Tower Hill, just beyond the gateway to the Tower. According to a report published in Paris, he gave a brief but nitric speech, saying, 'I die the king's good servant but God's first.'[17]

His life was over. But his legacy was only just beginning. For More's enduring achievement would turn out to be less his role as an embattled politician fighting for truth and justice against all the odds, in which capacity he had conspicuously failed, than as a heroic moral figure able to triumph from the grave.

Part 2

THE LEGACY

5

More's writings

Henry VIII maintained for the rest of his life that Thomas More had betrayed him. He regarded More's supporters as enemies of the State, making it suicide for anyone to contest the charges levelled against Thomas while the king was alive. In proof of his treachery, Henry claimed he had copies of More's letters from the Tower 'in charcoal and chalk when ink was not to be found'. They made it clear that Thomas had been plotting with Fisher against him.[1]

The first tentative steps to disprove these flimsy claims were taken by Thomas's eldest daughter Margaret before she died in 1544. She knew, as did More's favourite nephew, the printer William Rastell, that a collected edition of her father's writings and letters would be the best way to clear his name. More's own words could then speak for themselves. Her first step was to re-employ Thomas's faithful secretary, John Harris, who made accurate copies, in some cases from memory, of as many of More's letters and manuscripts as he could track down.

But when Henry died in 1547 and was succeeded by the nine-year-old Edward, his son by his third wife, Jane Seymour, things only got worse for the More circle. Cranmer took control of the boy-king's religious policy, coaxing Parliament into approving proposals for full-blooded Protestantism. More's supporters fled into exile on the Continent, settling mainly at Leuven and Douai.

When Edward died unexpectedly in 1553 of bronchial pneumonia (or possibly tuberculosis, the exact cause is disputed), Rastell's hopes of a collected edition of Thomas's writings improved exponentially. After the staunchly Catholic Mary Tudor took the throne and recalled her loyal kinsman Reginald Pole from exile in Rome to replace Cranmer, More's supporters returned home. Helped by his Catholic friends, Rastell first arranged for More's *Dialogue of Comfort against Tribulation* to be printed to test the market. It then took him four more long years to coordinate, and adequately finance, a syndicate of printers ready to publish the bulky folio needed for the collected works. Rastell's champion, the man who made all things possible, was Pole. His spiritual vision and understanding of the Reformation divide placed Thomas More at the very centre of a new Catholic drive to restore the old faith.

On 30 April 1557, *The Works of Sir Thomas More, Knight, Sometime Lord Chancellor of England, Written by him in the English Tongue*, running to 1,458 densely packed pages, was finally put on sale, complete with a dedicatory epistle from Rastell to Queen Mary, signalling the project's official status. The edition included all More's early English writings and works against heresy, and concluded with his writings from the Tower. The outstanding omission was *Utopia*, left out partly because it was in Latin, but chiefly because, in 1551, the forward Protestant Abraham Veale, who later collaborated with John Day, the printer of John Foxe's *Acts and Monuments* (or 'Book of Martyrs'), had published a bestselling translation by Ralph Robinson, then a clerk of the mint.[2] The sponsor was George Tadlow, a City haberdasher, Veale's friend and confidant.

Robinson's racy translation was to dominate the English market for *Utopia* until the mid-1960s. But it evolved in circumstances that made it differ significantly from More's original Latin text. The hottest topic in 1551 was the Protestant call for root-and-branch socio-economic reform following mass popular revolts in East Anglia and the south-west in 1549. A literalist reading of *Utopia* fitted perfectly with this endeavour. Also in 1551, a consortium of leading London merchants hoped to find investors for a proposed voyage to discover a north-eastern passage to Asia through the Arctic Ocean and the Bering Sea, in which they and several royal councillors planned to purchase shares. And it is easy to see how Hythloday's description of the island of Utopia and its inhabitants would have drummed up interest in this enterprise.

Robinson dedicated the first edition of his translation to Sir William Cecil, who had recently been sworn in as a privy councillor. A rising star, later chief minister to Queen Elizabeth I, Cecil stood at the hub of a Cambridge-trained, Protestant network that would come to bestride the political scene for almost 50 years. His name brought respectability to More's *Utopia* at a time when Thomas was very far from being a 'safe' author.

In his dedicatory epistle, Robinson praised More's 'incomparable wit', 'profound knowledge' and 'fine eloquence', but distanced himself from his 'blind' and 'obstinate' Catholicism.[3] Unfortunately, *Utopia*'s philosophical depth eluded Robinson. Despite More's abolition of social hierarchy in the work, Robinson reinstates it. Not only does he have 'magistrates' and 'citizens' on the island, but 'artificers', 'workmen', those who 'practise husbandry' and even 'companies of crafts'. Likewise, Robinson considered More's description of the Utopian cities to be too austere. To liven things up, he adds copious dashes of colour: his favourite word is 'gorgeous', so that whereas the essence of Utopian life and civic architecture is its simplicity, in his translation the streets and monuments of Utopia 'be of fair and gorgeous building', 'be very gorgeous ... of fine and curious workmanship', or have 'gorgeous and substantial arches'. The capital Amaurot is not merely an ironic analogue of London, it is indistinguishable from London itself.[4]

On the Continent, things were very different. After editions at Leuven in 1516, Paris in 1517 and Basel in March and November 1518, *Utopia* was published at Florence in its original Latin in 1519 by the printer Filippo Giunta at the end of a reprinted edition of More and Erasmus's translations of Lucian. And then Antonio Buonvisi, a silk merchant and banker from Lucca who traded in London and had known Thomas More for over 30 years, entered the scene. While More was a prisoner in the Tower, Buonvisi had sent him brewer's beer, stewed meat and a bottle of white wine every week, and in one of his final and most moving letters, Thomas described him as 'of all friends most trusty and to me most dearly beloved ... the apple of mine eye'.[5]

A few days after More's execution, Buonvisi returned briefly to Italy, taking with him some of More's papers and a copy of *Utopia*. Playing his cards skilfully, he wrote a series of letters to Thomas Cromwell which came to form one of Henry's main sources of news about troop movements, diplomacy and the ambitions of Francis I and Charles V, then battling for control of northern Italy. But beneath the veneer, Buonvisi was loyal to More: it was his house at Leuven that was to be the principal refuge for the surviving members of More's circle after their flight into exile.

At his ancestral villa of Forci near Lucca, Buonvisi drew his younger brother Vincenzo's attention to *Utopia*. Vincenzo, in turn, showed it to his friend Ortensio Landi, a young, radical intellectual trained in Bologna who had suffered exile in Lyon after flirting with the ideas of the reformers. Landi saw at once much of the true, enduring significance of More's work. Signing himself 'a citizen of Utopia', he popularized Thomas's ideas in 1544, arguing that civic life as it was conventionally understood in the corrupt European world is pointless. A truly wise man will retreat from it as he 'does not care about honours, he has contempt for glory and he refuses positions of power'. Only fools vie with each other to win political office in the hope of gaining wealth, honour and renown.

Landi considered *Utopia*, with its emphasis on ancient Greek values of 'justice' and 'equality', to have opened up a split between those fashionable political theorists advocating a return to Roman republican values of glory, honour and active citizenship as best seen in the age of Cicero, and those like Erasmus who advocated a return to earlier Greek ideas that were only made possible by the strict regulation of private wealth. In Italy, More's *Utopia* would be adopted as a model, not by the most popular theorists of the day with their ostentatiously Roman-driven values, but by their fiercest critics.[6]

Back in England, Rastell's decision to include so many of More's polemics against heresy in the *English Works* would have unintended effects. In Mary's reign, books like the *Dialogue Concerning Heresies*, *Apology* and *Debellation of Salem and Bizance* took on a fresh, immediate relevance. So intent were Mary and Pole to revive and enforce the heresy laws to their fullest potential, they would roast 284 Protestants alive in less than four years.

Then, after 1559, when Cecil talked Elizabeth into restoring Edward's Protestant Religious Settlement almost in full, Rastell's decision provoked an increasingly furious response from the Protestant martyrologist John Foxe. In his edition of the *Whole Works* of William Tyndale and Robert Barnes, Foxe treated More to a series of catcalls: he was 'a liar', 'a lying papist' and 'maliciously blind', a writer who 'blasphemeth God'.[7] And in his *Acts and Monuments*, Foxe cited 'credible witnesses' to accuse More of acting illegally. Instead of committing suspected heretics to the Tower or the bishop's prison, he had interrogated them at his house at Chelsea or imprisoned them in the stocks he kept in his gatehouse. To extract confessions, he several times resorted to violence, flogging suspects in his garden, one of them John Tewkesbury, whom he tortured with ropes until 'the blood started out of his eyes'.[8]

This, the most lurid of Foxe's accusations, was among several quietly retracted in 1570 when it was proved to be false, but it lived on regardless. In 1758, the Reverend Ferdinando Warner declared in *Memoirs of the Life of Sir Thomas More*:

> But amidst all the Encomiums which I think are due to the Memory of Sir Thomas More . . . I must not conceal from the Readers, what was a great Allay to all his Virtues, his furious and cruel Zeal in the Persecution of Hereticks.[9]

In a similar vein, More would be excoriated in 1820 by Charles Lamb, who pronounced More's polemics as 'penned with a wit and malice hyper-satanic'.[10]

In mid-Victorian England, Foxe's censures would be etched into the opening volumes of J. A. Froude's *History of England from the Fall of Wolsey to the Defeat of the Spanish*

Armada, which appeared in 1856 and marked the earliest academic history of Henry VIII's reign. More recently, similar accusations have reappeared in Jasper Ridley's *Thomas Wolsey and Thomas More: The statesman and the fanatic* (1982). According to Ridley, More's writings suggest that had he lived in the twentieth century, he would have justified the 'liquidation of millions of human beings as a regrettable but necessary measure', or else approved 'the extermination of three-quarters of the world's population by nuclear weapons'.[11] Not only is this flagrant hyperbole, it is anachronistic, because at the time More was lord chancellor, his duty to assist the bishops by arresting suspected heretics and enforcing capital sentences handed down by the church courts was laid down in an Act of Parliament of 1414.

It turned out that, apart from the unfinished English version of More's 'History of King Richard III', the most valuable and influential component of Rastell's edition of his uncle's writings would be Thomas's devotional treatises, prayers and unpublished letters from the Tower. One letter in particular, written in the summer of 1534 after Cromwell had granted Margaret leave to visit her father's cell in the hope that she could persuade him to take Henry's oath, stands out. It survives in no earlier copy than that made for Rastell's edition and is unique in that, ostensibly, it is an innocuous family newsletter sent by Margaret to her step-sister Alice Alington. In reality, Thomas and Margaret wrote it together, drawing on their combined ingenuity as they set out to justify to the world, and for posterity, why it was that More had no choice but to take his stand against Henry.

The letter takes the form of a dialogue between Margaret and her father and is a dramatic realization of what their exchanges might have sounded like had she really tried to coax him into swearing the oath. 'Conscience' is the key word, repeated over 40 times. The action is scripted as a temptation scene in which Margaret plays the part of 'Eve', which enables Thomas to play himself and deliver set-piece speeches on why and how he is equipped to resist tempta-tion. In a virtuoso performance in which the tension is relieved by pithy extracts from Aesop's fables, colloquialisms and laughter, More crystallizes for us his state of mind. Some people, he says, may imagine that in difficult cases the Scriptures or church doctrine are clear-cut, while others venture to differ, just as in one part or region of Christendom a law might be made that some think is lawful while others 'of equal learning and goodness' profoundly disagree. In such a doubtful case, no one can be bound 'upon pain of God's displeasure to change his own conscience' or be compelled to swear on oath that the 'local' law of a specific region or nation is valid 'standing his own conscience to the contrary'.[12]

It is, however, for *Utopia* that More is best known today. After such revolutionary fringe movements as the Levellers and Diggers had scandalized the property-owners of mid-seventeenth-century England with their strident demands for social equality, communally owned land and food and commodities freely distributed without the need for money, the pendulum swung towards interpreting *Utopia* more in terms of its religious than its social radicalism. In 1684, Gilbert Burnet, bishop of Salisbury, published a new transla-tion of *Utopia* that was a milestone in the process whereby More's reputation would be rehabilitated in Protestant circles. In his multi-volume *History of the Reformation* (1679–1714), Burnet used Hythloday's account of Utopian religion to reinterpret More as a Protestant *avant la lettre* who had called for radical reform of the Church and clergy ahead of Henry's break with the pope. By contrast, More could not have been serious in his apparent rejection of private wealth: such notoriously 'levelling' opinions were 'only intended to set many notions in his reader's way'.

Burnet's translation failed to oust Robinson's from its commanding market position, but for the first time made it possible to assimilate Thomas More to mainstream Anglicanism. Burnet continued to view More's later career as intoxicated by 'popery', but he could say that Thomas was the 'best man of the popish side in that age' on account of 'the integrity of his whole life, and the severity of his morals'.

With the Latin editions of *Utopia* all but forgotten and literalism ascendant, the stage was set for the reinvention of *Utopia* in the nineteenth century. Marx and Engels ranked More in *The German Ideology* alongside the Levellers, Owenites and Chartists as a forerunner of socialism. William Morris called *Utopia* 'a necessary part of a socialist's library'. And inspired by Marx, the Czech-born philosopher Karl Kautsky wrenched More's ideas from their context to argue for his 'modernity', based on his appreciation of the 'great principle' of socialism: that 'man is a product of the material conditions in which he lives'.

According to Kautsky, *Utopia*'s intellectual roots in Plato's *Republic* were beside the point. The 'constructive part' of *Utopia* sprang solely from the economic conditions of More's age. Utopian society had 'an essentially modern character', and its superficial resemblance to the *Republic* was 'only in externals'. More 'is one of the few who have been capable of this bold intellectual leap'.[13]

Marx's opinion of More held centre stage during the formative years of the Soviet Union, where, shortly after the 1917 Revolution, Lenin ordered an obelisk to be unveiled in Moscow's Alexandrovsky Gardens. Inscribed on it are 19 names, including those of Marx, Engels and (in Cyrillic script) 'T. More'.

From the mid-1960s onwards, new scholarly translations of *Utopia* have shifted the focus back to the spirit of More's original Latin text. In parallel, a run of scintillating studies by J. H. Hexter, Quentin Skinner and Eric Nelson among others have re-established the context of the work, arguing that, as with Erasmus in *The Praise of Folly*, More intended a radical critique of the values of his fellow intellectuals. As Skinner remarks, More 'believes that one of the most urgent tasks of social theory is to discover the root causes of injustice and poverty'. What is 'unique' about *Utopia* is that More 'follows out the implications of this discovery with a rigour unmatched by any of his contemporaries'. On the one hand, Renaissance intellectuals sought to deny that inherited wealth and ancient ancestry should be treated as qualifications for true nobility. On the other, they continued to defend the traditional link between these privileges and honour, reputation and political and social authority. *Utopia* is the book that asks 'whether we can really have it both ways'.[14]

6

Thomas More in art

Much of Thomas More's appeal today is visual, made possible by his distinctive legacy in art. In the autumn of 1526, when Thomas was helping Henry to write his *Letter in Reply to Martin Luther*, the supremely talented Augsburg-born portraitist Hans Holbein the Younger arrived penniless at Chelsea. Already Thomas had built up a small but impressive collection of oil paintings, coins and antique gems. At a glance he could appreciate the quality of Holbein's work – but not everyone else could yet. A genuine art connoisseur, More knew that wealthy patrons, except where religious paintings were concerned, still had only a dimly formed appreciation of the value of portraiture, preferring more opulent displays of tapestries, jewellery and gold and silver plate.

By the time Thomas had returned with Wolsey from Amiens in 1527, he had given Holbein two commissions to paint him. One was for a half-length oil portrait, now in the Frick Collection in New York, in which he would appear resplendent in his public capacity, wearing his official robes and golden chain with its 'S'-patterned badges signifying 'service' and allegiance to Henry. Holbein's second commission was for a more informal, life-sized family group portrait with More seated at the centre and his wife, father and children around him, to be painted on linen as a wall-hanging. He would still wear his gold chain, except this time, the 'S'-patterned badges would be shown back-to-front. Just as the Utopians had regarded gold as the most appropriate metal for urinals and forced criminals to wear gold rings in their ears and golden headbands, so More would invert his own collar.

In the single portrait, Thomas sits upright under a canopy, holding a letter or petition in his right hand. He stares straight past the viewer, his greyish-blue eyes focused intently on something in the distance. His expression is one of steely determination, or possibly of overwhelming sadness as he reflects on the storms in Christendom that he knew would come as a result of Henry's determination to marry Anne Boleyn.

The family group portrait, originally about 9 feet high and 12 feet wide, relied on water-based pigments and techniques of illusion and was to hang in the family's main reception space on the wall facing the door. On entering the room, the onlooker would then see the painting on the opposite wall before coming to stand in front of it. Substituted for the wall itself and even including a false door with a wooden portico to enhance the illusion, the picture would have conveyed a sense of gazing into a three-dimensional space where life-sized figures take their parts as if on a stage.

In preparation for these artworks, Holbein made a small collection of preliminary chalk drawings of individual sitters from life. The drawings still survive and have exerted a magical appeal ever since, in 1727, Queen Charlotte, wife of George II, rediscovered them with many more of Holbein's chalk drawings inside a bureau in Kensington Palace. Now locked safely away in special cabinets in the Royal Library at Windsor, they are exhibited in London from time to time or loaned elsewhere.

Another superlative artwork, a preliminary ink sketch of Holbein's original design for the family group portrait, annotated with some biographical information about each of the sitters and with More's requests for amendments to the composition, was sent as a gift by Thomas's eldest daughter Margaret to Erasmus in August 1528. This sketch is normally on show at the Kunstmuseum in Basel.

In the ink sketch and in a chalk drawing of More made specially for the family group scene, Thomas seems far more relaxed than in the oil painting. His expression is more animated, unguarded, enquiring, vulnerable, less bleak and remote. There is even a disarming hint of mirth, the suppressed smile of someone who finds the whole idea of posing for a portrait pleasantly ridiculous.

Unfortunately, we cannot say with any real precision what Holbein's finished version of the family group portrait looked like after More's amendments were incorporated and the final artwork hung on the wall at Chelsea, because it no longer exists. All we know with absolute certainty is that the painting showed More and some members of his family seated and others standing, several holding small books and all in poses that suggest they were about to begin family prayers. Among the more significant changes noted as having been requested in Holbein's sketch was that a pile of books should be scattered about the floor – untidily, but within easy reach of Margaret.

After More's execution in 1535, Holbein's finished wall-hanging was confiscated by Henry along with the rest of Thomas's property. Sometime during the 1570s it was bought by Andries de Loo, a Dutch art collector, and after changing hands several times was sold on to professional art dealers. It had reached the bishop of Olmütz's art collection at Kremsier Castle (now in the Czech Republic) by 1671, but in 1752 was destroyed in a disastrous fire.[1] Only the briefest record of it survives in a catalogue of paintings in Vienna.

At the time of More's death, however, his story as narrated through artworks was still in flux. In 1593, a fashionable artist of the second tier, Rowland Lockey, who could churn out portraits of Mary Queen of Scots and other historical notables by the yard and had once been apprenticed to the great Elizabethan portraitist and miniaturist Nicholas Hilliard, made various reproductions of the family group portrait. Of these, the two most important are full-sized versions in oils and on canvas, commissioned to more or less the same dimensions as the original Holbein work. One, until very recently, was a centrepiece of the Tudor and Stuart collection at the National Portrait Gallery in London.* The other is the property of the National Trust at Nostell Priory, near Pontefract, in Yorkshire.

When Andries de Loo died in 1590, one of Thomas More's grandsons, another Thomas More, seized his opportunity to buy back Holbein's original wall-hanging. A noted Catholic recusant who in 1586 had been imprisoned and interrogated by the notorious recusant-hunter and torturer Richard Topcliffe, this Thomas More lived at Low Leyton in Essex and had married another recusant, Maria Scrope. When he commissioned Lockey to paint a revised version of his grandfather's group portrait to hang in

---

* The painting is currently off display, and there are no immediate plans to rehang it after it returns from loan to an exhibition running from October 2016 to January 2017, as works on display are rotated. I am grateful to Neil Evans of the National Portrait Gallery for this information.

his own home, he lent the Holbein work to Lockey, who kept it for several months in his studio in Fleet Street in London.

No sooner had this Low Leyton branch of More's descendants commissioned their reproduction, the one owned by the National Portrait Gallery, than Thomas Roper, another of More's grandsons, the son of his daughter Margaret and her husband William Roper, gave Lockey his second commission. Thomas Roper had inherited the manor of Well Hall near Eltham in Kent from his father, and had married Lucy Browne, the aunt of Anthony Maria Browne, second Viscount Montague, one of the more active, if politically savvy, pillars of the Catholic cause in Elizabeth's reign.[2]

Unlike the Mores of Low Leyton, the Ropers of Well Hall liked to keep their heads down. William Roper had taken Henry VIII's oath of supremacy without the slightest hesitation. Surviving until 1578, he refused to attend Protestant services at his local parish church after Elizabeth was queen, but does not seem to have been fined. His son also sought relative anonymity: he was a loyal Catholic, but not actively committed to the reconversion of England like the Mores of Low Leyton.

But by the 1590s, both branches of More's descendants shared one important trait: they were bitterly anti-Jesuit. They were, in fact, in the vanguard of an increasingly influential movement that sought to distance English Catholics more generally from Pope Pius V's inflammatory decree of 1570 urging Catholics to depose Queen Elizabeth as a heretic schismatic tyrant. With few exceptions, the Jesuits backed the pope's decree, implicating themselves in a number of assassination plots against the queen and giving privy councillors and forward Protestants a golden opportunity to denounce all devout Catholics as traitors.

In revolt against such stereotyping, the More descendants spoke for a growing number of Catholic laity who pronounced themselves, in secular affairs at least, to be Elizabeth's loyal subjects. As time passed, they sought an accommodation with the government that would allow them some form of religious toleration in exchange for their political obedience. A crucial date is 1593: it was the year many Catholics faced up to the fact that Philip II's Armada of 1588 had failed and there was never likely to be a successful invasion of England.

A fresh appreciation of the life and career of Thomas More underscored this shift of opinion. As in *The Book of Sir Thomas More*, a Catholic play-script begun in or around 1593 that fell victim to censorship before its first performance despite its sponsors hiring William Shakespeare as a script doctor, More was Henry VIII's 'good and loyal servant'. He was a man whose moral fibre was considerably greater than that of the king who executed him for resisting his break with the pope.[3]

So widespread was this new outlook within the lay element of the Catholic community by 1593, it not only explains why the two different branches of More's descendants set about commissioning Lockey to paint fresh, updated versions of Holbein's wall-hanging, it explains why, once Lockey's reworkings were finished and safely hung at their patrons' houses, Holbein's original version was sold on again – this time to Thomas Howard, Earl of Arundel, a voracious collector of Holbein's original artworks. Incredible as it may seem today when Holbein's works are held in awe and the handful still in private hands command stratospheric auction prices, the fact is that by the mid-1590s, Holbein's original wall-hanging was *less* prized by More's descendants than their own new commissions. Quite simply, the new realizations told the story that the late-Elizabethan Catholic community wanted to hear.

So it was that in the Well Hall version of Lockey's painting, the one now hanging at Nostell Priory, the books Holbein had marked to be inserted on the floor in his preliminary ink sketch have disappeared, to be replaced by two dogs – symbols of 'fidelity'. Thomas More and his family kept a pet monkey, but no dogs: this is one of a myriad of small but discernible changes on the theme of 'loyalty' and 'fidelity'. And whereas in Holbein's original ink sketch we can only dimly observe two men seated, apparently reading, in the antechamber beyond the faux portico, in the Nostell Priory version one of them is identified and moved to a prominent position at the entrance to the portico. He is John Harris, Thomas More's faithful secretary, who now clasps a sword, a buckler and a sealed scroll.

Why Harris? Because he had been so central a figure in the transmission of More's literary legacy. His notebooks and memory had enabled Thomas's daughter Margaret and William Rastell, between them, to reconstruct those of More's original letters that were to be included in the great folio edition of the *English Works*.

Harris's sword and buckler refer to the annotations to Psalm 16 in the Catholic Reims-Douai translation of the Bible where the psalm is said to be:

> both a sword and buckler in affliction . . . Which holy David so composed, as was both convenient for himself, being molested with unjust afflictions by the wicked, and for any

other just person, or the whole Church in persecution, serving as a spiritual sword to strike the enemies, and as a shield
to bear of with patience and fortitude all their forces.[4]

'A just man's prayer in tribulation' is the head-note to the
psalm; patience in adversity is its message. Likewise, Harris's
scroll represents an enrolled copy of Henry VIII's letters
patent appointing 'his loyal servant Thomas More' to be his
lord chancellor.

Just as significantly, the book that More's daughter Margaret
is holding and about to read in the Nostell Priory painting
is clearly identifiable. In Holbein's ink sketch, we cannot
tell what this book is. But in Lockey's reworking, she holds
open on her lap two consecutive pages from the Chorus
of the fourth act in Seneca's *Oedipus*. Those pages cannot
be randomly chosen. They are Seneca's classic defence of
the 'middle way' or unambitious life, the passage in which
he counterpoints the security of lack of ambition with the
dangers of political engagement. His message is about the
relationship of human beings and fate. No one can predict
what will happen to those who enter the counsels of princes.
Fate is a kaleidoscopic series of causes and effects with which
not even the gods can interfere. Seneca was a favourite of
both Erasmus and Thomas More, the only Latin author
other than Cicero whom Hythloday was willing to recom-
mend in *Utopia*.

Almost certainly the Low Leyton version of the painting made explicit the text Margaret is about to read too.
Unfortunately, over the years, this version, the one now
belonging to the National Portrait Gallery, has been
damaged and restored. Any text that Lockey had once
included at the request of More's descendants or copied

from Holbein's now-lost wall-hanging to enable Margaret's book to be identified, as it can be at Nostell Priory, had already been erased before the damaged painting left its last private owner in 1935.

Other amendments requested by the Low Leyton branch of the family are still clearly visible. Several of Holbein's original sitters are omitted or shunted to the side to make way for Thomas More II who commissioned the painting, his wife Maria Scrope and two of their sons. They clasp Catholic missals in their hands, and the sons also hold up reliquaries. Until the painting was last cleaned and restored between 1971 and 1973, no fewer than eight Catholic heraldic shields identified these various sitters as clearly as if their names had been painted on to the canvas.

In two instances, this heraldry came complete with motto scrolls reading 'Christiano Catholico R[omano]: More'. The motto scroll has its origin in secular heraldry. Those on medieval arms and seals took their origins from the war-cry or *cri de guerre*, and in Scotland they were called slughorns or slogans. That 'Christiano Catholico R[omano]: More' has a provenance directly related to the Low Leyton branch of the More family is shown by a seal owned by Stonyhurst College in Lancashire. Engraved on a cornelian, it too has the motto 'Christiano Catholico R[omano]', and the accompanying heraldic arms are those of the Low Leyton branch of More's descendants – in the first and fourth quarters are a chevron and moorcocks, and in the second and fourth three lions rampant. The earliest member of the family to whom the seal can be traced is Thomas More II, the very patron who in 1593 commissioned Lockey to paint this particular example of the family group portrait.

Such heraldry was clearly designed to point the onlookers towards the controlling idea of the painting. After examining it in May 1972 at the National Portrait Gallery after its initial cleaning but before any more conservation work was begun, an independent heraldic expert stated that the heraldic arms dated from about the same time as the painting. An art expert was less certain, but was of the opinion that if they were added later, it was done long before any chemical change that affects certain pigments had begun.

Then, this painting suddenly became an example of the politics of art in a sense far removed from anything that might have been imagined in 1593. When the final restoration was undertaken between 1972 and 1973, five of the heraldic shields and both motto scrolls were obliterated. The restorer was instructed to leave intact the heraldic achievement of Maria Scrope's father, John, but to remove its associated shield. After consulting colleagues, a senior official of the Gallery, perhaps anxious that this painting should look as close as possible to Holbein's (and also to what he believed to be Lockey's) original vision of the work, wrote: 'Yes take them off – I've had a good look . . . they're horrid.'[5]

But by emasculating much of the heraldry in this artwork, especially the motto scrolls 'Christiano Catholico R[omano]', its quintessentially Catholic identity and cultural origins, so closely matched to a particular moment in the evolution of English Catholicism, were seriously compromised.

The tease is that, 40 years later, in August 2015, a room guide at a National Trust property, Montacute House in Somerset, where the painting was on temporary loan, noticed that in the background, above the heads of the sitters on the left-hand side of the composition, in exactly the right place, 'there are over-painted coats of arms (at least three)' finally peeping through into vision.[6] That surely creates room for hope that, in a future conservation, the overpainting may be removed and the iconographical integrity of this important artwork restored to something more approaching its original state.†

---

† I was last able to examine the painting at close quarters in 2011. At the time of writing, its unavailability, while off display, has prevented me from checking the subsequent changes to the pigments apparently used to overpaint the 'missing' heraldry and motto scrolls.

7

Canonization

Barely a year after Mary Tudor burned her first four Protestants in 1555, a campaign to secure Thomas More's
recognition as a Catholic martyr was set in motion. Reginald
Pole, who replaced Cranmer as archbishop of Canterbury,
was in the vanguard, asking his own right-hand man and
chief heresy-hunter, Nicholas Harpsfield, to write More's
official biography. Thomas's old friend Antonio Buonvisi
had recommended Harpsfield to Pole after getting to
know him in Leuven, where he had fled with More's other
supporters into exile in Edward's reign.[1]

   Since, however, Harpsfield was still studying at Oxford
in 1535 when More was executed, he needed help if he was
to write Thomas's life. He secured it from William Rastell
and William Roper, the best possible sources. Already Rastell
had begun writing a life of his uncle, although fragments
only of it now survive. Roper, widower of More's daughter
Margaret, was an even better informant, since he had
personally witnessed the key stages of Thomas's clash with
Henry. To put his testimony on record, Roper wrote a short
memoir for Harpsfield that he always claimed to be no
more than 'Notes' to show that his father-in-law, 'in his
days', had been accounted a man 'worthy [of] perpetual
famous memory'.[2] In fact, Roper's memoir is more pointed
and effective than the much longer manuscript Harpsfield
would produce. Roper did not write entirely from memory:

he several times refers to Rastell's forthcoming edition of More's collected works, so he must have owned a set of the proofs. He did sometimes put words into More's mouth. His account of More's trial is particularly suspect, since he had not been present. All the same, his memoir is a magnificent piece of writing, one of the finest early Tudor lives. It was first printed in 1626 at St Omer under the title *Life, Arraignment and Death of that Mirror of All True Honour and Virtue, Sir Thomas More.*

Harpsfield's life was longer because he ransacked the writings of Erasmus as well as More and drew heavily on the recollections of the exiles. He used the reports of More's trial that had circulated on the Continent, providing an impressively detailed account of More's arrest and last days. Far from concealing More's determined efforts to avoid death, he highlighted them, praising his patient resignation and faith in God when death was inescapable. The gist is that More's career was subverted by the corrupt desires of the tyrant Henry VIII. The break with Rome had been precipitated by his 'lusts'. More's heroic death was exemplary and has universal meaning for the true understanding of martyrdom. With an eye firmly fixed on the Vatican, Harpsfield concluded that Thomas had been martyred for a cause which 'toucheth religion and the whole faith'. It was a nobler cause than those for which earlier English saints who shared his forename had suffered. Astonishingly for a Catholic, Harpsfield ranked More as a worthier candidate for canonization than Thomas Becket had been when he was made a saint, on the grounds that Becket had merely defended the narrow jurisdictional claims of the papacy against royal power.[3]

But to extol More's claim to these giddy heights, one area of his life had to be doctored. As Harpsfield came closer to

71

completing the biography, he found that Mary's burnings had turned public opinion against her and Pole (and indeed Harpsfield himself): the result was that he came to discuss More's attitude to heresy solely from the viewpoint of his writings on the topic. At no point did he seek to refute Protestant accusations of illegality and torture. More the heresy-hunter was airbrushed out of the story, making the overall effect somewhat anodyne.

When Elizabeth took the throne, the tables were turned. Stripped of his posts for refusing the new queen's oath of supremacy, Harpsfield was sent to the Fleet Prison, where he was kept in solitary confinement until the year before his death. His biography of More had most likely been finished in 1557, and almost certainly by 1559, when it was presented to Roper as a New Year's gift. But it stayed in manuscript until 1932, when the Early English Text Society printed it. The distinguished Catholic historian Eamon Duffy has suggested the explanation may lie in divisions within the Marian regime itself: many who had sworn Henry's oath of supremacy still occupied high office in Mary's reign, notably Richard, now Lord Rich, who had given the fatal evidence at More's trial, and afterwards become a major player in the Marian burnings in Essex.

With the Protestants ascendant, the effort to promote the cause of More and Fisher moved to the Continent, where in 1582–3 Pope Gregory XIII implicitly approved their cults by allowing a magnificent fresco by Niccolò Circignani depicting their executions to be included in a cycle of martyrdom frescos in the chapel of the English College in Rome.[4] Destroyed by vandals at the beginning of the nineteenth century, the fresco is known from an engraving published in 1584. These were years in which an increasingly confident papacy sought to reassert its authority over local and national churches after the traumatic events of the Reformation. In 1588 Sixtus V, a pope famous for his mistrust of Philip II of Spain and his penchant for throwing crockery about when in a temper, went on to approve the first new round of canonizations since the Council of Trent.

Full of hopes for More's canonization, Thomas Stapleton, an inspirational leader of the Catholic exiles at Leuven and Douai and a man who had consciously rejected the siren call of the Jesuits, began his own biography of Thomas More. Evolving out of a sermon he had preached at Douai in 1586, the work was the concluding part of a trilogy entitled *Tres Thomae* ('Three Thomases') in which the other saints' lives were those of St Thomas the Apostle and Thomas Becket. The book's polemical force lay in this juxtaposition. Publication came at a critical time for Catholics – just as the Spanish Armada was preparing to sail up the English Channel.[5]

Stapleton's energy not only breathed new life into the cause of Thomas More's canonization, it significantly refocused his appeal away from the more aggressively political preoccupations of the Jesuits and more towards those of ordinary lay recusants in ways soon to be realized in Lockey's paintings. For Stapleton argued that while More was unquestionably a hero of conscience, he was never a rebel. Rather, he was the victim of an unjust law, which he violated 'neither by word or deed'. 'This law, moreover, concerned religion and not the policy of the State.' Although he had been unbending, he had not challenged the law or criticized anyone who had accepted it. He condemned neither Henry's oath nor the Act of Supremacy: 'he merely kept silence for conscience's sake'.[6]

Stapleton failed in his main aim. When Elizabeth survived in the long war against Philip II, to be succeeded in 1603 by the Protestant James VI of Scotland, Rome lost interest in More and the English martyrs. Their cause was largely forgotten until after Catholic Emancipation in 1829. Within a decade of Pope Pius IX's restoration of the Catholic church hierarchy in 1850, however, the baton was taken up, in turn, by Cardinals Wiseman and Manning. Renowned for boldly affirming papal infallibility at the First Vatican Council of 1869–70 and for urging Catholics to close ranks against the encroachments of the State in Italy and elsewhere, Manning began the 'ordinary process' of sending a long list of names for beatification to the Vatican.

And, eventually, it worked. On 29 December 1886, the anniversary of the murder of Thomas Becket at Canterbury in 1170, a carefully selected date, Pope Leo XIII beatified More and Fisher, along with 52 other Englishmen (a majority of them Jesuit missionary priests) put to death between 1535 and 1583. This meant their names could be added to the list of those whom the Catholic Church counts as 'Blessed' and their cults and shrines could be venerated in England, if not yet throughout the world.

Attempts to persuade Pope Pius XI to canonize More and Fisher began three years ahead of the centenary of Catholic Emancipation. At their Low Week conference in 1926, the Catholic bishops agreed to press ahead on the grounds that More and Fisher were pre-eminent among the English martyrs and it would be a great boost to Catholic morale if they could be canonized.[7]

Bishop Peter Amigo of Southwark took the lead, visiting Rome to canvass support, after which a none-too-subtle campaign of leafleting and letter-writing was undertaken to convince Catholics – hopefully non-Catholics too – of the essential loyalty of these two virtuous Englishmen despite their resistance to the king. In Rome, a willing and experienced postulator was found in Fr Agostino della Vergine. Meanwhile in England, Fr Philip Hallett, rector of St John's seminary at Wonersh in Surrey, undertook the task of translating Stapleton's life of More into English, for which he was named vice-postulator and given the daunting task of assembling the arsenal of historical evidence that would be needed at Rome to justify More's claim.

The wheels ground fine and slow. By 1929, all Hallett could achieve of any real significance was a public exhibition of books, relics, portraits and copies of historical documents relating to Thomas More, open for a week in Chelsea at the convent of a French order of sisters, the Congregation of Adoration Réparatrice. There, as an accompanying leaflet explained, 'the Blessed Sacrament is exposed day and night and prayers continually offered for the conversion of England'.

It was precisely the risk of appearing to be lobbying for the nation's reconversion that troubled Bishop Amigo, who strenuously sought to block moves in that direction lest the canonization bid should provoke an Anglican backlash. From the outset, too, a serious obstacle to advancing the cause was the need to show that More and Fisher had worked miracles. (Two miracles, well authenticated, are normally needed before a saint is canonized.) Despite appeals to the faithful to send in their evidence, nothing of substance could be found.

Petitioned in June 1930, the Congregation of Rites in Rome gave its approval for the cause to proceed. This was despite vocal objections from Cardinal Laurenti, the Prefect, who argued that More and Fisher should not be fast-tracked ahead of the other English martyrs. A certain Mgr Salotti circumvented this opposition by approaching Pope Pius directly. But the absence of miracles still stood in the way. 'I have great faith and hope', reported Fr Agostino, 'that the English can provide good miracles so that we can soon have the joy of seeing these glorious martyrs elevated.'

Over the next five years, Agostino wrote regularly to Bishop Amigo (usually in Spanish in which both men were fluent), describing the progress of the cause. Mostly the issue was money. Twice a year, Agostino warned, fees had to be paid to the Congregation of Rites, and should the cause succeed, the prospective ceremonies at Rome could not conceivably cost less than 250,000 lire (around £5,000 then, worth £100,000 today). This did not include the expenses of repairing some portion of the fabric of St Peter's basilica. (Whenever a canonization took place, some renovation work had to be paid for.) As Agostino quipped, mixing Latin and Spanish, *sine pecunia no se hace nada* ('without money nothing is done'). The trouble was that English funds were low, leading Agostino to complain, 'I need more money . . . much more money.' The archives now at Archbishop's House in Southwark are peppered with such appeals, culminating in a dramatic telegram from the rector of the English College in Rome, saying 'Agostino needs 3500 pounds immediately – Smith'.

A breakthrough came in July 1934, when Pope Pius personally intervened. He asked Cardinal Laurenti to inform Amigo that old transcripts of the English State Papers sent to Rome by Cardinal Manning had been discovered and that the Historical Section at the Vatican had been ordered to study them. The pope dropped a hint that if these old papers were sufficiently convincing, he might perhaps dispense with the need for miracles.

By early December, the Historical Section had finished its investigations and was ready to report. 'I have great confidence that the case will succeed', chirruped Agostino excitedly, 'because the Holy Father wants to please the English people and has a great interest in advancing the matter.'

Advised by Agostino that the Congregation of Rites was to meet again on 29 January in a plenary session in the presence of the pope, Amigo set out for Rome, where he entered a formal plea for the canonization. The verdict of the Historical Section was favourable, and in a rare ironic twist the Promoter of the Faith (popularly known as the 'Devil's Advocate') supported the canonization instead of challenging it. Although no precedent could be found, he said, for going forward to a full public canonization in St Peter's without miracles, the evidence of martyrdom was in this case strong enough to make an exception.

On 1 February the pope ruled in favour of the canonizations. On the 10th the papal decree was read in the presence of Britain's representative to the Holy See and the ambassador to Italy, and in March an official announcement followed that no miracles would be required. Pope Pius, it was said, had been 'profoundly moved by the ardent devotion towards these blessed martyrs'. At once, Agostino made another urgent appeal for funds as costs were now double his original estimate: 'Send me £4000, which I must put on deposit', and when no reply was received, 'For St Peter's we need 270,000 lire: apart from this amount, there is the cost of illuminating the cupola and façade which Mgr Pellizzo puts at 50,000 lire and says he could do for 40,000.'

And again, on 28 April, 'I need 500,000 lire', a sum that did not include gratuities.

The canonizations took place in a spectacular candlelit ceremony at St Peter's on Sunday, 19 May 1935, which was a great success despite squabbles over the ticketing in the basilica. (English pilgrims had been allocated over 400 of the most prized seats, but on arrival found many of their places stolen by Italians and Germans.) The Vatican was unusually anxious about British press coverage, and to ensure a sufficient presence of notables other than clergy had invited the Speaker of the House of Commons, the chancellors of the universities of Oxford and Cambridge and the chancellor of the exchequer. All refused to attend. According to a leading Catholic lawyer and privy councillor, Lord Russell of Killowen, the chancellors of both universities had faced implacable opposition from their governing bodies. 'It is', he added, 'very tiresome.' Stanley Baldwin, shortly to be prime minister for the third time, also declined to attend. Then the second figure in the National Government, he lived at 11 Downing Street, even though Neville Chamberlain was chancellor of the exchequer. (Baldwin was also chancellor of Cambridge, so it is not clear whether his refusal was in that capacity or on behalf of the government.) Lord Killowen was especially irked to be forbidden by the lord chancellor to attend the canonizations in a personal capacity.

The canonizations were hardly welcomed with open arms by the British establishment, but the only overt hostility came from members of the Protestant Truth Society. Anglicans were divided, some claiming More and Fisher 'for their own', others condemning them as traitors. Possibly after reading Burnet's translation of *Utopia* or his skewed account of More as a Protestant *avant la lettre* in his *History of the Reformation*, the novelist Rose Macauley went so far as to suggest that More and Fisher were 'Renaissance Anglicans'.

To Amigo's great relief, *The Times* had printed an enthusiastic leader the moment the pope's approval of the canonizations was known. On 2 February, the paper declared the matter to be one for celebration. More and Fisher would be the first Englishmen to be recognized as saints since the Reformation and 'before the fourth centenary of their death comes round'. 'Their work was done and their mark was left in institutions that have remained for four centuries at the core of the national life, in Parliament, in the Law Courts, in the Universities.' More, in particular, through his *Utopia* and other writings, had 'contributed greatly . . . to the foundation of English literature'. With Hitler in power in Germany and Stalin in Russia, the troubled world of the 1930s might draw the moral that 'the men who suffer for conscience still pass the ultimate judgement upon their persecutors'.

Nothing was said publicly about any plans among the more zealous members of the Catholic elite for the conversion of England. Amigo's tactic of silencing this extreme minority section of opinion had been successful. It was lucky for him that, in July 1934, his letter of thanks to the pope for offering to refer Cardinal Manning's old dossier of State Papers to the Historical Section at the Vatican was not leaked. For besides reassuring Pius that 'Catholics and non-Catholics in England are proud of these two outstanding Englishmen – nobody would think of them as traitors to King or Country', he went on to add, 'I am sure that these Martyrs are praying for the conversion of England.' That remark played extremely well in Rome. Had it become known at home, there would have been an outcry. For in spite of a rapid drift towards secularization after the First World War, Britain was still extremely wary of the threat of resurgent 'popery'. Any link between 'popery' and the cause of the conscientious objector or whistle-blower in society could have proved lethal.

8

The lure of fiction

By the 500th anniversary of Thomas More's birth in 1978, his popularity had soared to dizzy heights. At the time of his canonization, his chief advocates had been drawn almost exclusively from the Catholic elite. Now, the leader-writer of *The Times* could confidently say, 'If the English people were to be set a test to justify their history and civilization by the example of one man, then it is Sir Thomas More whom they would perhaps choose.' The claims of King Alfred, Elizabeth I, Shakespeare, Gladstone and Churchill were fleetingly considered, but the laurels went to More. To clinch the point, the paper's editor commissioned a series of features to highlight his 'lasting inspiration'.[1]

Needless to say, this extraordinary cultural shift was inspired less by historical fact than by creative fiction. In July 1960, a remarkable play about Thomas More's moral stand against Henry VIII's oppression had opened at the old Globe Theatre in London and transferred to Broadway. Written by Robert Bolt and called *A Man for All Seasons*, the play was an instant triumph. So successful was it, it became the top choice for sixth-form dramatic societies in schools across Great Britain, trumping Shakespeare's *Twelfth Night*, and Columbia Pictures bought the film rights. Bolt was eager to direct the film himself, but Columbia insisted on an experienced Hollywood insider. They chose Fred Zinnemann, a veteran Oscar-winner with such classics under his belt as *High Noon* and *From Here to Eternity*.

Paul Scofield took the lead role in both the play and the film. In the film, Robert Shaw was Henry VIII and Susannah York was More's eldest daughter Margaret. Vanessa Redgrave made her Hollywood debut in a walk-on part as Anne Boleyn. Released in 1966, the film was nominated for eight Oscars and won six, retaining its position at or near the top of the box office in Britain and the USA for almost a year, until nudged aside by the James Bond thriller, *Casino Royale*. According to *Variety*, the trade journal of the US entertainment industry, the film was 'proof' that a film 'without sex, violence or songs' could hit the jackpot.[2]

Zinnemann's film turned Thomas More into a household name. The 1960s was the perfect moment for a story of the kind Bolt wanted to tell. In Britain, these were years made famous by the Beatles, the rise of feminist, gay and lesbian rights movements and by sometimes violent sit-ins organized by the Campaign for Nuclear Disarmament. In the USA, the Civil Rights and anti-Vietnam War movements were at their peak. It was the era of the Cold War and the Cuban Missile Crisis. In Washington DC, memories of McCarthyism were still fresh. Such topics as the relationship of the individual to the State and the power of the State over the individual sparked heated debates, even sometimes riots, on university campuses. Terms of abuse regularly voiced from the US far right included 'draft dodger' and 'conscientious objector'.

Bolt tapped into this fault-line in society with considerable acumen, turning More into a lone voice standing up for the rights of the individual. 'Society', he explained in his Preface to the play, can only have as much idea as we have what we are about, for it has only our brains to think with. And the individual who tries to plot his position by reference to our society finds no fixed points, but only the vaunted absence of them.[3]

Bolt's title for the play came from More's contemporary Robert Whittinton, one of the network linked to Thomas's old Greek tutors William Grocyn and Thomas Linacre. In a school grammar textbook, Whittinton had set the following translation exercise for his students:

> More is a man of an angel's wit and singular learning. He is a man of many excellent virtues . . . I know not his fellow. For where is the man . . . of that gentleness, lowliness and affability. And as time requireth, a man of marvellous mirth and pastimes, and sometime of sad gravity, as who say 'A Man for All Seasons'.[4]

As Bolt continued in his Preface, he had taken a Christian saint and refashioned him as a sculptor might remodel a lump of marble or bronze to suit his dramatic purposes, turning him into 'a hero of selfhood'. More, he confessed, 'became for me a man with an adamantine sense of his own self. He knew where he began and left off.' Crisis befell him only when he was asked to retreat 'from that final area where he located his self'. Then, 'this supple, humorous, unassuming and sophisticated person set like metal, was overtaken by an absolutely primitive rigour, and could no more be budged than a cliff'.

All this makes for thrilling drama, but thoroughly misrepresents the way that the historical Thomas More understood the role of 'conscience'. The crux is the point in the play and the film where, in a rare moment of passion, More says to the Duke of Norfolk, who has questioned the doctrine of the apostolic succession of the pope: 'what matters to me is not whether it's true or not but that I believe it to be true, or rather not that I *believe* it, but that *I* believe it.'

This definition of conscience is, historically, not More's at all, but Luther's. The idea of the autonomous conscience was a notion chiefly invoked by Anne Boleyn and Cranmer to justify the king's divorce campaign. At the point at which More resigned the chancellorship, Henry was relaying this idea to all who would listen. He argued that the pope could lawfully be resisted when a man was guided by 'conscience' or 'private law' as written in his heart by the Holy Spirit after reading the Bible. 'Conscience' set a man free. Its dictates must be obeyed, especially when a man discovered that his marriage was against God's law. As Cranmer summed things up, 'we must obey our conscience: and in other things the Church'.[5]

This was an idea the real-life Thomas More found utterly repellent, especially if this view of 'conscience' was to be imposed on other people. As he well knew from his time confuting Luther, it was the heretics who quoted specific texts of Scripture in the particular senses in which they understood them to justify moral decisions. Scripture had to be interpreted by the whole Church: teasing out the true meaning was a matter not for individuals, but for the 'consensus of Christendom', often arrived at over many centuries. One's own moral convictions, however sincere, might be erroneous, just as those of the heretics were.[6]

This was not a message the public wanted to hear, and Bolt's success in transforming the way the world looks at Thomas More was proved conclusively by the speech given on 14 January 1999 by Congressman Henry Hyde, the Chairman of the Judiciary Committee of the House of Representatives, at the opening of President Bill Clinton's impeachment trial following the Monica Lewinsky affair. Hyde's speech was transmitted live on TV and radio and streamed on the internet. Most of the next day's newspapers highlighted the references to More. Even in Scotland, where the national Parliament was about to convene for the first time since 1707, the headline crowed: 'TV Nation raised on Oprah Winfrey watches bemused as Sir Thomas More takes the stand'.[7]

Hyde (as he believed) quoted More's words in the Tower to his eldest daughter: 'When a man takes an oath, Meg, he's holding his own self in his own hands.' No one noticed that these were never More's words; they were Bolt's, word for word out of the play. No one noticed, because, by then, as the distinguished Harvard professor Richard Marius had explained in 1989, 'people already knew what we were supposed to find when we studied More. We were supposed to find Robert Bolt's More.'[8] The masterfully taut dialogue of Bolt's script and Zinnemann's magical deployment of light during the River Thames scenes – actually filmed on the Norfolk Broads – had made this so. Such subtleties compensated ten times over for the embarrassment – in the film – of the crudely painted plywood façade of Hampton Court palace.

Then, in 2009, like a thunderbolt, came the publication of Hilary Mantel's Booker Prize-winning novel *Wolf Hall*, an entirely different work of creative fiction from Bolt's, that would send More's stock plunging to its all-time low. As the *Los Angeles Times* put it,

It's Sir Thomas More ... who truly goes through the shredder. So, you thought More was the valiant, dignified saint from *A Man for All Seasons*, the hero of conscience prepared to stand up to secular powers and die for his faith? Alas, no.[9]

Of course, all good stories need a baddie. As Anthony Trollope explains in *Barchester Towers*, 'it is ordained that all novels should have a male and a female angel, and a male and a female devil'.[10] In *Wolf Hall*, Thomas More is the male devil, Anne Boleyn the female. Anne, who enjoys cunnilingus with her brother on the side, sets out to trap a hen-pecked, naive and prissy king who has a murderous temper and needs regular sex, but underperforms in bed. More, in Mantel's creation, is 'some sort of failed priest', a heretic-hunting torturer straight out of the pages of John Foxe's *Acts and Monuments*, a self-flagellating Catholic zealot armed with a whip and manacles, whose perverted mind exploits human weaknesses as a sport. He marries an illiterate wife so he can mock her at dinner parties. He is unhealthily obsessed with his eldest daughter Margaret (there is the faintest hint of incest). He likes animals, but only if they're caged.

Henry's infatuation for Anne sets in motion a kaleido-scopic, deadly competition for power and influence. The old medieval divisions into those who fight, those who pray and those who labour have been made irrelevant by the printing press, votes in Parliament and the availability of consumer goods. A century earlier Cromwell and More would have fought with swords, but in Henry's brave new world they duel with words. After More raids Humphrey Monmouth's house in search of Lutheran books, he says to Cromwell, 'Not come to see us yet, Master Cromwell? ... Come now, my tongue is sharper than you deserve. We must be friends, you know.' The invitation is plainly a threat.

More's execution follows a treason trial at which Cromwell rigs the jury but protests he hadn't (and maybe wishes it too). But the major confrontation is before that in the

Tower. Thomas Audley, Henry's new lord chancellor and Cromwell's sidekick, begins questioning More:

> 'Let us be clear. You will not take the oath because your conscience advises you against it?'
>
> 'Yes.'
>
> 'Could you be a little more comprehensive in your answers?'
>
> 'No.'
>
> 'You object but you won't say why?'
>
> 'Yes.'
>
> 'Is it the matter of the statute you object to, or the form of the oath, or the business of oath-taking in itself?'
>
> 'I would rather not say.'
>
> Cranmer ventures, 'Where it is a question of conscience, there must always be some doubt . . .'
>
> 'Oh, but this is no whim. I have made long and diligent consultation with myself. And in this matter I hear the voice of my conscience clearly.' He puts his head on one side, smiling. 'It is not so with you, my lord?'

It would be Mantel's talent for conjuring up something more or less approximating to the authentic speech patterns of the characters that would have reviewers lining up to applaud. It is, continued the *LA Times* reviewer, almost as if, in another life, Mantel had been 'a stenographer taking notes in the taverns and palaces of Tudor England'. A speech from More that follows his tussle with Audley over the oath earns this high praise. For Mantel shows us a Thomas More considerably more attuned to the nuances of the Catholic view of 'conscience' than Bolt's. As More counters:

> You say you have the majority. I say I have it. You say Parliament is behind you, and I say all the angels and saints are behind me, and all the company of the Christian dead,

for as many generations as there have been since the church
of Christ was founded, one body, undivided.

Cromwell cannot see it. 'A lie', he retorts, 'is no less a lie
because it is a thousand years old.' Audley, on the other hand,
just seems to think that More's answers prove his pride,
malice and invincible sense of moral superiority. This, after
all, is a man who (in Mantel's realization) can never resist
the urge to mock. He will even snigger at a humble clerk
for making a mistake in his Latin.

Whereas Mantel's More is a sneering, conceited, mis-
ogynist bigot of the worst sort, a pantomime villain born
with a silver spoon in his mouth, her Cromwell is the very
opposite. Supremely artful and insinuating, cultured and
multilingual, but also a man who knows how to turn a
knife so as to kill a man silently, we know almost from the
novel's earliest pages that he will succeed. Son of a Putney
blacksmith who beats him up, he is a meritocrat with a
vision of change that belongs in the real world rather
than in Utopia, a man who transcends social class and is
one of the 'brethren' (meaning a clandestine Protestant). A
workaholic and master of spin, he loves dogs and children,
and understands human frailty. He has blood on his hands,
but we might just start to like him.

Historical accuracy, naturally, is never the issue. This is
a novel. What counts, as the eminent Harvard professor
Stephen Greenblatt remarks, is 'the illusion of reality, the
ability to summon up ghosts'. 'Lock Cromwell in a deep
dungeon in the morning', Mantel has Thomas More tell
us, 'and when you come back that night, he'll be sitting on
a plush cushion eating lark's tongues, and all the gaolers
will owe him money.' Quite so.[11]

Writing for the *London Review of Books*, Professor Colin Burrow, a doyen of the British literary scene and world expert on the English novel, neatly captured what he calls 'the brilliance and perhaps the perversity of *Wolf Hall*'.

> Mantel's chief method is to pick out tableaux vivants from the historical record . . . and then to suggest that they have an inward aspect which is completely unlike the version presented in the history books. The result is less a historical novel than an alternative history novel.

She also plays games on her readers.

> Repeatedly, *Wolf Hall* suggests that no one, apart from Cromwell, can really know what will turn out to be important. Its chief running joke is that people and things which come to be of immense historical significance are within the novel unobserved and peripheral.[12]

Thus, when More arrests Monmouth on suspicion of heresy and searches his house, Mantel lays down a trail that will bring about a poignant end to her story. Taken from the Tower to be executed on Tower Hill after his trial, Thomas is escorted to the scaffold by Monmouth, elected in June 1535 as sheriff of London. 'Monmouth is too good a man to rejoice in the reversal of fortune. But perhaps we can rejoice for him?' says someone. Is it Cromwell or Mantel speaking? We cannot be sure. What we do know is, historically, this is fantasy. For the sheriffs of London and Middlesex, for any particular year, did not come into office until Michaelmas Day (29 September). More died in July, and so Monmouth was not yet sheriff then – the previous year's sheriffs, sworn in to their posts in 1534, were still officiating and it would be one of those who presided at the execution. For the simple-minded historian, it is all just too neat. Nowhere is there a sense of Thomas's tragedy – that it had been Henry himself who had set his old secretary on to confuting Luther and the reformers and then pulled the rug from under him.

In the end, More's representation in fiction becomes a zero-sum game. What his popularity and influence gained from Bolt has been demolished by Mantel. The trouble is that fiction is often so very believable. As Melanie McDonagh commented in the *London Evening Standard* after *Wolf Hall* won the Booker Prize, 'because it's so readable, so convincing, it risks being taken as a true version of events. And that's scary.'[13]

Epilogue

On 31 October 2000, ironically Reformation Day, Pope John Paul II published an apostolic letter proclaiming Thomas More to be the patron saint of politicians and people in public life. At a millennial moment, the letter explained, 'it is helpful to turn to the example of Saint Thomas More, who distinguished himself by his constant fidelity to legitimate authority and institutions precisely in his intention to serve not power but the supreme ideal of justice'.[1]

The move received a mixed welcome. Several journalists mischievously pointed out that there was a patron saint for everything, even for cobblers and shoemakers. And a champion of William Tyndale spoke his mind: 'Is it wise – is it Christian?' he asked, 'to remind politicians of a man who held his incinerated opponents to be "well and worthily burned"?'[2]

In the end, an assessment of Thomas More has to struggle with two thorny questions. Did he, first of all, mean what he said in *Utopia*? So far, we have hedged our bets by referencing Hythloday and the interlocutor 'Thomas More' to opposing sides of More's divided consciousness. That, undoubtedly, is the largest part of the story, but in the final reckoning, we have to ask whether Hythloday's vision of justice and equality was also the real-life More's.

It may well have been. In 1519, three years after *Utopia*'s publication, a Carthusian monk, John Batmanson, went so far as to accuse Erasmus of heresy outright for publishing his edition of the Greek New Testament. Instantly More leaped to the defence of his friend in a 14,000-word tirade.

This time, however, he found himself drawn into justifying the relevance of Greek values to the contemporary world. 'God showed great foresight', he says,

> when he instituted that all things should be held in common ... for not only does everyone love his own plot of land or his own money, not only does everyone cherish his own family or his own set of colleagues, but to the extent that we call anything our own it absorbs our affections and diverts them from the service of the common good.[3]

More, here, speaks from obvious conviction. The vision he expresses of society is one like Plato's in the *Republic* in which everything is held in common and the citizens live in a perpetual state of happiness and felicity, as in Utopia.

In *Wolf Hall*, Mantel's Cromwell voices the obvious riposte.

> Let's have this straight. Thomas More here will tell you, 'I would have been a simple monk, but my father put me to the law. I would spend my life in church, if I had the choice. I am, as you know, indifferent to wealth. I am devoted to things of the spirit. The world's esteem is nothing to me.'

Cromwell pauses for a few seconds before delivering his punch line. 'So how did he become Lord Chancellor? Was it an accident?'

Mantel has a point. For all his apparent disdain for worldly goods, More enjoyed the trappings of success: his Chelsea estate, his library, his coin and antique gem collections, his paintings. So why did he not sell them and give the money to the poor? The answer, plausibly, is that they gave him pleasure, and in Plato's philosophy there was a different definition of 'equality' from the one we have today. It held – in a curious anticipation of George Orwell's 'some animals are more equal than others' – that some citizens are more equal too.

Plato's ideal was always that the republic should be ruled by the best minds of the age. His theory is dimly echoed in Rousseau's remark that the ordinary citizen must be 'forced to be free'. There were two kinds of 'equality': an 'arithmetical' sort in which all citizens were mathematically equal, and a 'geometric' kind that justified the rule of 'guardians' or 'wise and good men'. Democrats favoured the first of these, Plato emphatically the second.[4]

Plato never expected his ideal society to be realized on earth, and the same is true of More, whose final words in *Utopia* are 'I freely confess that in the Utopian commonwealth there are very many features that in our own societies I would wish rather than expect to see.' By describing their ideal commonwealths, Plato and More meant to map out like cartographers the ancient Greek values they believed were the only possible way to mitigate the evils and corruptions of power. Since Thomas More lived in England, which was a monarchy, not a republic, *Utopia*'s message is that 'the best state of a commonwealth' is when a ruler with instincts approaching those of a philosopher-prince is advised by councillors of 'true nobility' ('true' based on intellect and wisdom) who nudge him ever closer to a fairer, more just society given the adverse conditions of real life. The problem with this approach is that it smacks of champagne socialism.

The other thorny question is the apparent schizophrenia created by More's dual roles as author of *Utopia* and inquisitor in heresy cases. Clearly anachronism has to be stripped out of the debate. When More was lord chancellor, his duty to defend the Church from heretics and enforce the church courts' sentences was defined in an Act of Parliament. That is an unpalatable fact. And while any civilized person since the Enlightenment knows that burning people alive is morally and profoundly wrong, both Catholics and Protestants in the sixteenth century justified capital punishment in flagrant cases of heresy and apostasy. Cromwell used Henry's new legislation to kill far more defiant Catholics than More killed evangelical Protestants.

What is unique about Thomas More, a layman not a priest or bishop, is his zeal and the way he felt he needed to publicize his loathing towards the heretics in his epitaph. Not only did he boast that he had been 'grievous to thieves, murderers and heretics', he had the epitaph etched in stone and its text transcribed in a letter to Erasmus that he knew would almost immediately be published. The stone was placed on the family tomb he had constructed in Chelsea Old Church, and over time became a considerable embarrassment. So much so that, when the monument was restored, the wording was truncated and a gap left in the marble. Since 1795, a visitor to Chelsea has been able to discover only that More had been 'grievous to thieves and murderers'.[5]

What are the lessons of More's political career? Quite simply, his model is the exact opposite of Disraeli's 'damn your principles, stick to your party' – the maxim encapsulating the political system in almost all present-day democracies. He was the first politician in British history to make ethical principles the *raison d'être* of a public career, without regard to his personal safety. And he appealed to universal values of truth, justice, freedom and conscience in the face of what he saw to be an increasingly tyrannous State.

The uncomfortable loose end is that he applied these values differently if anyone questioned the doctrine or authority of the universal Catholic Church while he was in power. He had his reasons. But for those Protestants who refused to recant, as later for More himself, there could be no freedom except in heaven.

Glossary

abjure   to renounce on oath, retract, recant

Catholic Emancipation   the relaxation of the restrictions on Catholics most obviously achieved by the Roman Catholic Relief Act of 1829

Chartists   members of a working-class democratic movement from 1838 to 1858 that aimed to achieve political reform chiefly by constitutional means

court of chancery   the lord chancellor's court, which could make exceptions to strict legal rules so as to reach the fairest possible decisions

court of star chamber   a high court dealing chiefly in allegations of serious crime at which the judges were the king's councillors

declamation   a rhetorical exercise or speech, usually on a paradoxical or riddling topic, put into the mouth of a mythical or historical figure

Diggers   a small group of social revolutionaries who in 1649–50 called for a free commonwealth and argued that land should be held in common

duchy of Lancaster   the department that administered the lands and revenues brought to the Crown in 1399 by Henry Bolingbroke when he deposed Richard II and usurped the throne

enclosures   the practice whereby greedy landlords enclosed or fenced off fields formerly used for growing crops so that they could be used for grazing sheep, leading to widespread redundancies in the workforce

Eucharist   the sacrament of the Lord's Supper or Holy Communion

exchequer   the king's chief financial department with special responsibility for audit and accounting

excommunication   exclusion from the communion and fellowship of the Church

groom of the stool   the chief gentleman of the king's privy chamber, the most intimate (and politically important) royal body servant, usually also keeper of the king's privy purse in charge of the king's personal funds and who met his day-to-day expenditure

indictment   a legal document setting out the accusation in a criminal trial

interlocutor   one who takes part in a dialogue or conversation

Levellers   a populist movement during the 1640s that called for an extended suffrage and social equality

lord chancellor   the king's chief legal officer, usually a leading councillor

nuncio   a papal ambassador

Owenites   followers of Robert Owen (1771–1851), a Welsh social reformer and one of the founders of the cooperative movement

postulator   the person who in the Roman Catholic Church pleads the cause of a candidate for beatification or canonization

privy chamber   the innermost apartments at Court where the king lived and worked, staffed by trusted body servants who strictly controlled access

pursuivant   a royal or state messenger with the power to enforce arrest warrants

recusant a person (Catholic) who after the Elizabethan Religious Settlement of 1559 denied the royal supremacy or refused to attend services in the local parish church

sacrament one of seven solemn ceremonies of the Catholic Church whereby grace is conveyed to the believer

undersheriff a permanent official who advised the sheriffs and sat as judge in the sheriff's court

Notes

1 Shaping a mind

1 J. Woolfson, *Padua and the Tudors* (Cambridge: James Clarke, 1998), pp. 39–72, 103–18.

2 *The Correspondence of Erasmus*, ed. R. A. B. Mynors, D. F. S. Thomson and others, 16 vols (Toronto: University of Toronto Press, 1974–), VII, p. 19.

3 *The History of King Richard III and Selections from the English and Latin Poems*, ed. R. S. Sylvester (London and New Haven: Yale University Press, 1976), pp. 158–9.

4 The 'failed monk' explanation of More's life and career is most strongly argued by Richard Marius, *Thomas More* (New York: Harvard University Press, 1984), pp. xxii–iii, 34–43, 464–5.

5 *Correspondence of Erasmus*, VII, p. 21.

6 *A Dialogue of Comfort against Tribulation*, ed. F. Manley (London and New Haven: Yale University Press, 1977), p. 86.

7 *History of King Richard III and Selections from the English and Latin Poems*, pp. 130–6.

8 National Archives, SP 1/239, fos 223–4.

2 *Utopia*

1 *The Correspondence of Erasmus*, ed. R. A. B. Mynors, D. F. S. Thomson and others, 16 vols (Toronto: University of Toronto Press, 1974–), VII, pp. 23–4.

2 In pursuing these arguments, I am much indebted to two mould-breaking articles by Eric Nelson: 'Greek nonsense in More's *Utopia*', *Historical Journal*, 44 (2001), pp. 889–917; '*Utopia* through Italian eyes: Thomas More and the critics of civic humanism', *Renaissance Quarterly*, 59 (2006), pp. 1029–57.

3 *St Thomas More: Selected letters*, ed. E. F. Rogers (London and New Haven: Yale University Press, 1961), p. 73. See also J. M. Parrish, 'A new source for More's "Utopia"', *Historical Journal*, 40 (1997), pp. 493–8.

4 Here I follow Nelson; see n. 2 above.

5 *St Thomas More: Selected letters*, pp. 6–64.

6 J. H. Hexter, *More's 'Utopia': The biography of an idea* (Princeton: Princeton University Press, 1952), p. 21.

7 *Correspondence of Erasmus*, III, pp. 234–5.

3 The king's servant

1 C. Curtis, 'More's public life', in *The Cambridge Companion to Thomas More*, ed. George M. Logan (Cambridge: Cambridge University Press, 2011), pp. 74–6. For Henry's advice, see *The Correspondence of Sir Thomas More*, ed. E. F. Rogers (Princeton: Princeton University Press, 1947), p. 495.

2 *Letters and Papers, Foreign and Domestic, of the Reign of Henry VIII*, ed. J. S. Brewer and others, 21 vols in 32 parts, and *Addenda* (London: HMSO, 1862–1932), III. i, no. 1284.

3 Corporation of London Record Office, MS Repertory 5, fos 199^v, 204.

4 *The History of King Richard III and Selections from the English and Latin Poems*, ed. R. S. Sylvester (London and New Haven: Yale University Press, 1976), pp. 95–6.

5 Information on Gambara is from J. Sharkey, 'The politics of Wolsey's cardinalate, 1515–1530', Cambridge Ph.D. (2008), pp. 118–56.

6 *The Complete Works of St Thomas More*, VI: *A Dialogue Concerning Heresies*, ed. T. Lawler and others (London and New Haven: Yale University Press, 1981), Pt 1, pp. 331–42.

7 *Complete Works*, VI, Pt 1, pp. 152, 200, 236, 243, 346, 374–66, 405–10. See also *Complete Works*, VIII: *The Confutation of Tyndale's Answer*, ed. L. A. Schuster and others (London and

New Haven: Yale University Press, 1973), Pt 1, pp. 226–7, 262–3; Pt 2, pp. 766–7.

4 The dissident

1 *St Thomas More: Selected letters*, ed. E. F. Rogers (London and New Haven: Yale University Press, 1961), pp. 206–9.
2 *St Thomas More: Selected letters*, pp. 209–10.
3 *St Thomas More: Selected letters*, pp. 171–2.
4 The evidence can be followed up in John Guy, *A Daughter's Love: Thomas and Margaret More* (London: Harper Perennial, 2008), pp. 192–8, 310–13; Richard Rex, 'Thomas More and the heretics: statesmen or fanatic?', in *The Cambridge Companion to Thomas More*, ed. George M. Logan (Cambridge: Cambridge University Press, 2011), pp. 93–115.
5 *St Thomas More: Selected letters*, pp. 178–83.
6 *The Lyfe of Sir Thomas Moore knighte, written by William Roper*, ed. E. V. Hitchcock, Early English Text Society, Original Series, 197 (London: Early English Text Society, 1935), p. 57.
7 *The Complete Works of St Thomas More*, IX: *The Apology*, ed. J. B. Trapp (London and New Haven: Yale University Press, 1979), pp. 168–9.
8 *St Thomas More: Selected letters*, pp. 216–23.
9 For the circumstances of publication, see Chapter 5.
10 *A Dialogue of Comfort against Tribulation*, ed. F. Manley (London and New Haven: Yale University Press, 1977), pp. 30, 114, 129–30, 184, 193, 292, 300–2.
11 *Letters and Papers, Foreign and Domestic, of the Reign of Henry VIII*, ed. J. S. Brewer and others, 21 vols in 32 parts, and *Addenda* (London: HMSO, 1862–1932), V, no. 1292.
12 *St Thomas More: Selected letters*, pp. 249–50.
13 National Archives, SP 2/R, fo 20 (formerly fo 24). See also *Letters and Papers*, VIII, no. 814 (i).
14 *Letters and Papers*, IV. ii, no. 2639.

15 National Archives, SP 2/R, fos 20 (bottom)–21 (formerly fos 24–5).

16 *Lyfe of Sir Thomas Moore knighte, written by William Roper*, p. 248. See also *St Thomas More: Selected letters*, p. 252; J. Duncan M. Derrett, 'The trial of Sir Thomas More', *English Historical Review*, 79 (1964), pp. 449–77.

17 'The Paris newsletter', printed in N. Harpsfield, *The life and death of Sir Thomas Moore, knight, sometymes Lord high Chancellor of England*, ed. E. V. Hitchcock, Early English Text Society, Original Series, 186 (London: Early English Text Society, 1932), appendix 2, p. 266.

5 More's writings

1 *State Papers during the Reign of Henry VIII*, 11 vols, Record Commission (London: Record Commission, 1830–52), VII, pp. 633–6 (copies available at all major research libraries or via <http://sources.tannerritchie.com/browser.php?bookid=1416>).

2 New editions followed in 1556, 1597, 1624 and 1639, culminating in editions of 1869, 1887, 1893, 1910 and 1929.

3 *A fruteful, and pleasaunt worke of the beste state of a publyque weale, and of the newe yle called Vtopia* (London, 1551), sig. +iii^v–iv (copies available at the British Library, Guildhall Library, Bodleian Library).

4 See J. Binder, 'More's *Utopia* in English: a note on translation', in *Essential Articles for the Study of Thomas More*, ed. R. S. Sylvester and G. Marc'hadour (Archon: Hamden Books, 1977), pp. 229–33.

5 *St Thomas More: Selected letters*, ed. E. F. Rogers (London and New Haven: Yale University Press, 1961). pp. 254–6.

6 Landi considered *Utopia* to be so important that he translated it into Italian, publishing it at Venice in 1548. See L. Firpo, 'Thomas More e la sua fortuna in Italia', in *Studi sull'Utopia, Raccolti da Luigi Firpo*, ed. Firpo (Florence: L. S. Olschki, 1977), pp. 31–58; P. F. Grendler, 'Utopia in Renaissance Italy: Doni's "New World"', *Journal of the History of Ideas*, 26

(1965), pp. 479–94; Eric Nelson, '*Utopia* through Italian eyes: Thomas More and the critics of civic humanism', *Renaissance Quarterly*, 59 (2006), pp. 1041–52.

7 See E. Evenden and T. S. Freeman, *Religion and the Book in Early Modern England: The making of Foxe's 'Book of Martyrs'* (Cambridge: Cambridge University Press, 2011), p. 245.

8 *The Acts and Monuments of John Foxe*, ed. G. Townsend, 8 vols (London, 1843–9), IV, p. 689 (copies available at all major research libraries or in another, searchable edition with largely the same pagination via <https://archive.org/details/texts?and[]=Townsend%20%22john%20Foxe%22>). For related accusations, see *The Acts and Monuments of John Foxe*, IV, pp. 643–52, 664, 670–1, 688–94, 697–707; V, pp. 3–11, 18–26, 29, 99–100, 181.

9 F. Warner, *Memoirs of the Life of Sir Thomas More* (London, 1758), pp. 67–8 (copies available at the British Library, Bodleian Library, Cambridge University Library).

10 *The Indicator*, 63 (20 December 1820).

11 J. Ridley, *The Statesman and the Fanatic: Thomas Wolsey and Thomas More* (London: Constable, 1982), pp. 292–3.

12 *The Correspondence of Sir Thomas More*, ed. E. F. Rogers (Princeton, NJ: Princeton University Press, 1947), pp. 514–32.

13 K. Kautsky, *Thomas More and his Utopia with a Historical Introduction* (London: A. & C. Black, 1927), especially pp. 1–3, 97–8, 160–2, 172, 190, 248–50.

14 Q. Skinner, *The Foundations of Modern Political Thought*, 2 vols (Cambridge: Cambridge University Press, 1978), I, pp. 255–62; Skinner, 'Sir Thomas More's *Utopia* and the language of Renaissance humanism', in *The Languages of Political Theory in Early Modern Europe*, ed. A. Pagden (Cambridge: Cambridge University Press, 1987), pp. 154–5.

6 Thomas More in art

1 See L. Lewis, *The Thomas More Family Group Portraits after Holbein* (Leominster: Gracewing, 1998), pp. 1–5.

2 For the connections of More's descendants with key Elizabethan Catholic kinship networks, see M. Questier, 'Catholicism, kinship and the public memory of Sir Thomas More', *Journal of Ecclesiastical History*, 53 (2002), pp. 476–509.

3 *The Book of Sir Thomas More*, ed. W. W. Greg (Oxford: Malone Society, 1961); P. W. M. Blayney, ' "The Booke of Sir Thomas Moore" re-examined', *Studies in Philology*, 69 (1972), pp. 167–91; T. Merriam, 'The misunderstanding of Munday as author of *Sir Thomas More*', *Review of English Studies*, New Series, 51 (2000), pp. 540–81; G. Melchiori, '*The Booke of Sir Thomas Moore*: a chronology of revision', *Shakespeare Quarterly*, 37 (1986), pp. 291–308.

4 See *The holie Bible faithfully translated into English, out of the authentical Latin. Diligently conferred with the Hebrew, Greeke, and other editions in diuers languages*, 2 vols (Douai, 1609–10), II, p. 38 (copies in the British Library, Bodleian Library, Cambridge University Library).

5 All information about this restoration comes from the conservation file ('Registered Packet') for NPG 2765 now preserved in the Heinz Archive and Library of the National Portrait Gallery. I have in my possession an official copy of the full colour transparency of the painting made in 1971 before any cleaning or restoration work had begun.

6 See <http://www.npg.org.uk/collections/search/portrait/mw01734/ Sir-Thomas-More-his-father-his-household-and-his-descend ants?LinkID=mp06288&search=sas&sText=Thomas+More& OConly=true&role=sit&rNo=3> (accessed 24 August 2016).

7 Canonization

1 E. Duffy, *Fires of Faith: Catholic England under Mary Tudor* (London and New Haven: Yale University Press, 2009), pp. 180–6.

2 *The Lyfe of Sir Thomas Moore knighte, written by William Roper*, ed. E. V. Hitchcock, Early English Text Society,

Original Series, 197 (London: Early English Text Society, 1935), p. 197.

3 N. Harpsfield, *The life and death of Sir Thomas Moore, knight, sometymes Lord high Chancellor of England*, ed. E. V. Hitchcock, Early English Text Society, Original Series, 186 (London: Early English Text Society, 1932), p. 214.

4 Anne Dillon, *The Construction of Martyrdom in the English Catholic Community, 1535–1603* (Aldershot: Ashgate, 2002), pp. 174–7.

5 *The Life and Illustrious Martyrdom of Sir Thomas More*, ed. P. E. Hallett (London: Burns, Oates and Washburne, 1928). See W. Sheils, 'Polemic as piety: Thomas Stapleton's *Tres Thomae* and Catholic controversy in the 1580s', *Journal of Ecclesiastical History*, 60 (2009), pp. 74–94. Later editions of Stapleton's work appeared at Cologne and Graz in 1612 and 1689. Versions were also included in editions of More's *Latin Works* which appeared after 1620.

6 *The Life and Illustrious Martyrdom of Sir Thomas More*, pp. 226–7.

7 My information for the remainder of this chapter comes from Archives of the Catholic Archdiocese of Southwark, unsorted boxes R71.1, R76.1. As yet, these papers are unlisted: researchers must sift through both boxes to find the more important letters and documents. I gratefully acknowledge the help of the archivist, Jenny Delves, in making these papers available for me to study and for allowing me to quote from them. See also Michael Clifton, *Amigo, Friend of the Poor: Bishop of Southwark, 1904–49* (Leominster: Gracewing, 2006), pp. 127–38; J. Davies, 'A cult from above: the cause for canonisation of John Fisher and Thomas More', *Recusant History*, 28 (2007), pp. 458–74.

8 The lure of fiction

1 *The Times*, leader (7 February 1978).
2 J. R. Nicholl, 'More captivates America: the popular success of *A Man for All Seasons*', *Moreana*, 13 (1976), pp. 139–44.
3 R. Bolt, *A Man for All Seasons* (London: Methuen, 1960), pp. xi–xii.
4 *Vulgaria Roberti Whit[t]intoni Lichfeldiensis* (London, 1520), fo xvᵛ (copy available at the Henry E. Huntington Library, San Marino, California; copies of slightly different editions of the same date are located at the John Rylands University Library of Manchester and St John's College, Cambridge).
5 *The Divorce Tracts of Henry VIII*, ed. E. Surtz and V. Murphy (Angers: Moreana, 1988), pp. 267–9.
6 *The Complete Works of St Thomas More*, V: *Responsio ad Lutherum*, ed. J. M. Headley (London and New Haven: Yale University Press, 1969), Pt 1, pp. 301–5, 413–17, 627–9; Pt 2, pp. 733–45; *The Correspondence of Sir Thomas More*, ed. E. F. Rogers (Princeton: Princeton University Press, 1947), p. 525; B. Gogan, *The Common Corps of Christendom: Ecclesiological themes in the writings of Sir Thomas More* (Leiden: Brill, 1982), pp. 244–7, 267, 291, 363–5. See also P. Marshall, 'Saints and cinemas', in *Tudors and Stuarts on Film: Historical perspectives*, ed. S. Doran and T. S. Freeman (London: Palgrave Macmillan, 2009), pp. 46–59.
7 *The Scotsman*, news report by Tim Cornwell (15 January 1999).
8 Marshall, 'Saints and cinemas', p. 53.
9 *Los Angeles Times*, review by Ross King (8 October 2009).
10 Anthony Trollope, *Barchester Towers* (London: Vintage Classics, 2015), p. 254.
11 *New York Review of Books* (5 November 2009).
12 *London Review of Books* (20 April 2009).
13 *London Evening Standard* (17 September 2009).

Epilogue

1 'Apostolic letter', in *Thomas More: Why patron of statesmen?*, ed. T. Curtright (Lanham: Lexington Books, 2015), appendix, pp. 197–201.

2 See 'Aftermath', in B. Moynahan, *Book of Fire: William Tyndale, Thomas More and the bloody birth of the English Bible* (London: Abacus, 2011).

3 *The Complete Works of St Thomas More*, XV: *Letter to Martin Dorp, Letter to the University of Oxford, Letter to Edward Lee, Letter to a Monk*, ed. D. Kinney (London and New Haven: Yale University Press, 1986), p. 279; translation from E. Nelson, '*Utopia* through Italian eyes: Thomas More and the critics of civic humanism', *Renaissance Quarterly*, 59 (2006), p. 1038.

4 P. Cartledge, *Democracy: A life* (New York: Oxford University Press, 2016), pp. 99–100.

5 D. Lysons, *The Environs of London: being an Historical Account of the Towns, Villages and Hamlets within Twelve Miles of that Capital: II, County of Middlesex* (London, 1795), pp. 83–4 (copies available at the British Library, Bodleian Library, Cambridge University Library).

Further reading

Biographies

The best early memoir of Thomas More is William Roper's, conveniently found in *Two Early Tudor Lives: The life and death of Cardinal Wolsey by George Cavendish; The life of Sir Thomas More by William Roper*, ed. R. S. Sylvester and D. P. Harding (London: Yale University Press, 1962). Modern biographies include Peter Ackroyd, *The Life of Thomas More* (London: Vintage, 1998), and John Guy, *A Daughter's Love: Thomas and Margaret More* (London: Harper Perennial, 2008). Anthony Kenny's brief *Thomas More* (Oxford: Oxford University Press, 1983) is especially adept at explaining More's view of conscience. Other lives include R. W. Chambers, *Thomas More* (London: Jonathan Cape, 1935), but the work obliterates More's role against the heretics. A shrewd, but hostile psychological profile is Richard Marius, *Thomas More* (New York: Harvard University Press, 1984).

General works

A short recent introduction to Henry VIII's reign is John Guy, *Henry VIII: The quest for fame* (London: Allen Lane, 2014). Richard Rex, *Henry VIII and the English Reformation* (London: Palgrave Macmillan, 1993) is a valuable survey for students. The most distinguished, readable full biography of Henry VIII is still J. J. Scarisbrick, *Henry VIII* (London: Eyre & Spottiswoode, 1968).

More's writings

Utopia

Paperback translations capturing much of the tone and texture of More's masterpiece are *Utopia*, ed. George M. Logan, trans. Robert M. Adams (3rd edn; Cambridge: Cambridge University Press, 2016); *Utopia*, ed. Clarence H. Miller and Jerry Harp (2nd edn; London and New Haven: Yale University Press, 2014); and *Utopia*, ed. Paul Turner (London: Penguin Classics, 1983). For students, the most up-to-date and astute annotation and brief commentary can be found in Logan's third edition.

Other writings

For modern critical editions of all More's writings, scholars are indebted to the *Yale Edition of the Complete Works of St Thomas More*, ed. R. S. Sylvester, C. H. Miller and others, 15 vols (London and New Haven: Yale University Press, 1963–97). More's letters are published in *The Correspondence of Sir Thomas More*, ed. E. F. Rogers (Princeton: Princeton University Press, 1947). A modern selection is *St Thomas More: Selected letters*, ed. E. F. Rogers (London and New Haven: Yale University Press, 1961). Yale paperbacks also include *The History of King Richard III and Selections from the English and Latin Poems*, ed. R. S. Sylvester (London and New Haven: Yale University Press, 1976), and *A Dialogue of Comfort against Tribulation*, ed. F. Manley (London and New Haven: Yale University Press, 1977). Currently the best, most accessible edition of More's *Richard III* is *The History of King Richard III: A reading edition*, ed. George M. Logan (Bloomington and Indianapolis: Indiana University Press, 2005).

Specialist works

An invaluable guide to Thomas More's life and writings, summarizing the latest research, is *The Cambridge Companion to Thomas More*, ed. George M. Logan (Cambridge: Cambridge University Press, 2011). For the broader context of *Utopia* in Renaissance political thought, see Quentin Skinner, *The Foundations of Modern Political Thought* (2 vols, Cambridge: Cambridge University Press, 1978). Invaluable essays on *Utopia* include Quentin Skinner, 'Sir Thomas More's *Utopia* and the language of Renaissance humanism', in *The Languages of Political Theory in Early Modern Europe*, ed. A. Pagden (Cambridge: Cambridge University Press, 1987), pp. 123–57, and E. Nelson, '*Utopia* through Italian eyes: Thomas More and the critics of civic humanism', *Renaissance Quarterly*, 59 (2006), pp. 1029–57. J. H. Hexter, *More's 'Utopia': The biography of an idea* (Princeton: Princeton University Press, 1952) remains a classic.

More's role as a king's councillor is helpfully explored by Cathy Curtis in *Cambridge Companion*, pp. 69–92, and in greater detail by John Guy in *A Daughter's Love: Thomas and Margaret More* (London: Harper Perennial, 2008), pp. 112–215. Richard Rex assesses More's stand against the heretics in *Cambridge Companion*, pp. 93–115, where several myths are dispelled. More's view of the legality of heresy proceedings is defended by H. A. Kelly, 'Thomas More on inquisitorial due process', in *English Historical Review*, 123 (2008), pp. 847–94.

Fully documented accounts of More's collision with Henry VIII and interrogations at Lambeth and in the Tower can be found in G. R. Elton, *Policy and Police: The enforcement of the Reformation in the age of Thomas Cromwell* (Cambridge: Cambridge University Press, 1972) and in Guy, *A Daughter's Love*, pp. 229–64. For a sympathetic discussion of More's devotional writings in the Tower, see L. L. Martz, *Thomas More: The search for the inner man* (London and New Haven: Yale University Press, 1990).

More's trial is brilliantly reconstructed by J. Duncan M. Derrett in 'The trial of Sir Thomas More', *English Historical Review*, 79 (1964), pp. 449–77, and 'Neglected versions of the contemporary account of the trial of Sir Thomas More', *Bulletin of the Institute of Historical Research*, 33 (1960), pp. 202–23. Derrett's work is complemented but not superseded by *Thomas More's Trial by Jury: A procedural and legal review*, ed. H. A. Kelly and others (Martlesham: Boydell & Brewer, 2011).

Cardinal Pole's role in More's legacy is discussed by Eamon Duffy in *Fires of Faith: Catholic England under Mary Tudor* (London and New Haven, CT: Yale University Press, 2009), pp. 178–86. Other aspects of More's literary legacy are explored by Anne Lake Prescott in *Cambridge Companion*, pp. 265–87. His legacy in art is assessed by L. Lewis, *The Thomas More Family Group Portraits after Holbein* (Leominster: Gracewing, 1998). See also D. R. Smith, 'Portrait and counter-portrait in Holbein's "The Family of Sir Thomas More"', *Art Bulletin*, 87 (2005), pp. 484–506; K. Wells, 'The iconography of Saint Thomas More', *Studies (Ireland)*, 70 (1981), pp. 55–71.

The most helpful guides to the campaign for More's canonization are Anne Dillon, *The Construction of Martyrdom in the English Catholic Community, 1535–1603* (Aldershot: Ashgate, 2002); Michael Clifton, *Amigo, Friend of the Poor: Bishop of Southwark, 1904–49* (Leominster: Gracewing, 2006); J. Davies, 'A cult from above: the cause for canonisation of John Fisher and Thomas More', *Recusant History*, 28 (2007), pp. 458–74.

Robert Bolt's play-script is published with an illuminating Preface by the author. See Bolt, *A Man for All Seasons* (London: Methuen, 1960). An informative commentary by Peter Marshall entitled 'Saints and cinemas' is in *Tudors and Stuarts on Film: Historical perspectives*, ed. S. Doran and T. S. Freeman (London: Palgrave Macmillan, 2009), pp. 46–59. P. I. Kaufman's article 'Dis-Manteling More', in *Moreana*, 47 (2010), pp. 165–93, attempts to correct Hilary Mantel's wrong facts, but this exercise partly misses the point as her book is a novel. A subtler assessment of *Wolf Hall* is 'How to twist a knife' by Colin Burrow in the *London Review of Books*, 31 (30 April 2009), free online at <http://www.lrb.co.uk/v31/n08/colin-burrow/how-to-twist-a-knife>.

Index

113

Index

Index

Index